GRIEVING THE UNEXPECTED
The Suicide of a Son

Grieving the Unexpected
THE SUICIDE OF A SON

DR. GARY LeBLANC

Essence
PUBLISHING

Belleville, Ontario, Canada

GRIEVING THE UNEXPECTED
The Suicide of a Son
Copyright © 2003, Gary LeBlanc

All Scripture quotations, unless otherwise specified, are from *The Holy Bible,
New International Version*. Copyright © 1973, 1978, 1984 International Bible
Society. Used by permission of Zondervan Publishing House. All rights reserved.

Scripture quotations marked KJV are from *The Holy Bible, King James Version*. Copyright © 1977, 1984, Thomas Nelson Inc., Publishers.

National Library of Canada Cataloguing in Publication

LeBlanc, Gary, 1941-

  Grieving the unexpected : the suicide of a son / Gary LeBlanc.

Includes bibliographical references.

ISBN 1-55306-448-8.—ISBN 1-55306-490-9 (LSI ed.)

        1. Suicide—Psychological aspects. 2. Bereavement—Psychological
aspects. 3. Children—Death—Psychological aspects. . LeBlanc, Gary, 1941-
I. Title.

HV6548.C3L42 2002   155.9'37'092   C2002-905767-1

Essence Publishing is a Christian Book Publisher dedicated to furthering the
work of Christ through the written word. For more information, contact:
44 Moira Street West, Belleville, Ontario, Canada K8P 1S3.
Phone: 1-800-238-6376. Fax: (613) 962-3055.
E-mail: info@essencegroup.com
Internet: www.essencegroup.com

*To my wife, Peggy (Margaret), and
my son, Neil, and daughter, Jaclyn, without whose
support, love and encouragement this
book would not have been possible.*

Shawn Darrell LeBlanc
(1971-1999)

Table of Contents

Acknowledgements

THE IDEA for a book about what I have experienced as the result of Shawn's death, and the idea that it may be of help to others, was first planted in my mind by John Weiler, an area minister for the Atlantic Convention of Baptist Churches who was at a men's breakfast presentation I gave almost a year after losing Shawn. His encouraging words started a process that resulted in an article which appeared in the September/October 2000 issue of *Faith Today*. I am very grateful for the help and support of Larry Matthews, the Managing Editor of *Faith Today* at that time. This book is a continuation of that initial project.

I am also very grateful to my colleagues at Atlantic Baptist University for their constant affirmation and their practical help in granting me a half-year sabbatical to work on the manuscript. The emotional toll on me was such that I doubt I could have completed it without the time away from regular duties.

To Steve Dempster and Bill Morrison, colleagues at Atlantic Baptist University; Jim Beverley, professor at Tyndale Seminary, Toronto, Ontario; Mike Kaye, social worker and pastor, Brantford, Ontario; Bob Beverley, therapist and pastor in New York; and Larry Barlow, therapist and administrator, Tallahassee, Florida; for their willingness to read the manuscript and give insightful feedback which has been so appreciated. I have benefited greatly from their input.

Finally, I want to acknowledge the wonderful support and love of my family and friends. Peg, Neil and Jaclyn, to whom this book is dedicated, gave strength and comfort to me in the midst of their own grief, for which I will always be grateful. As well, marvelous friends, many of whom I mention in this book, encouraged and sustained me in those most difficult times and continue to do so. They have been used as God's loving instruments of grace and caring, enabling me to live in hope and faith even in the shadow of such a loss, for which I thank my Lord.

Preface

WRITING THIS account has been an emotional roller coaster for me as never in my wildest dreams did I ever imagine such an event happening in our family. My training as a family sociologist and therapist prepared me to help other families in crisis, but it never occurred to me I could be on the receiving end of such a crisis and would need help from others that I was trained to provide. I am so thankful the Lord, through His people, surrounded us with His sustaining grace.

But the death of my son, especially in the way it happened, has shaken me to my very foundations, initiating a difficult and soul-searching process. It has caused me to question my faith, my role as a father and my viability as a teacher. It has forced me to examine closely much of what I previously took for granted, to reexamine the unimportant things I took so seriously and reevaluate more crucial considerations like friendship, to which I sometimes gave much less attention than was deserved.

The preciousness of life and the value of each day have been impressed on my being like never before, especially when I realize that some days and activities can never be repeated. Thus, we grieve for what can never be. What a shame that we may not realize just how precious and valuable some things are until we no longer have the option of experiencing them.

But I have learned much from what has happened, even though I still feel the price has been far too high. How I wish another learning vehicle could have been used. However, I am grateful for the lessons learned, even from such a terrible event. I have learned much about God's sustaining grace, strength and comfort; I have learned much about God's methodology for comforting His children; I have learned much about the incredible value of family and friends as God's instruments of care. I hope some of this has been communicated well in this book and that perhaps some hurting person may find help and comfort in these pages.

Introduction

FOR MOST of us, our life experience has taught us that living in a fallen world has its hardships, troubles and heartaches, even for the child of God, and we should not be surprised when we suffer painful trials (1 Peter 4:12). We all struggle with tribulations of many kinds. However, life can also impact us with the unexpected, those events which stun and overwhelm us, which come crashing in on us like a tornado leaving us shocked and numb, for which we can never be adequately prepared. For the LeBlanc family, January 1999 was such a time. On January 7, 1999, I had a biopsy that revealed I had prostate cancer. Even though it was in its earliest stages and an operation would almost surely be successful, it was a shock to say the least as all the tests had indicated that cancer was only a remote possibility. But the events of Thursday, January 28, 1999 would make the previous news pale in comparison. The day gave no warning of what was in

13

store as, given the circumstances, everything seemed normal with our world. This account is the story of what happened that day and our subsequent journey through incredible pain and healing in coping with the most devastating event that can befall a family.

I went to my office that morning at Atlantic Baptist University in Moncton, New Brunswick, Canada, and Peg, my wife, was at home getting ready for her curling match at 1:00 p.m. Our eldest son, Shawn, aged twenty-seven, came by the house late that morning as was his custom and, upon leaving at about noon, told Peg he had some errands to run. As he was in the midst of setting up a small business, this was quite normal. I arrived home a few minutes after Shawn left, disappointed I had missed him as I wanted to arrange a lunch date with him for the following day to talk about how things were going. We did this periodically, and it was always an enjoyable time. However, I decided I would stop by his apartment after taking Peg to her curling match as I had some time before a doctor's appointment at 2:00 p.m. We were running a bit late, so I decided I would drop by Shawn's after my appointment.

I met with my family doctor to discuss my cancer diagnosis which had been made by the urologist to whom I had been referred. I wanted to enquire about the urologist's competence, his skill as a surgeon and other matters such as if I would be better off going to another hospital. The news was very reassuring, so I left the doctor's office much relieved and drove over to Shawn's apartment. As my compact truck, which he was using, was there, I assumed he was home. I knocked at the door but got no response. It was a beautiful day, sunny and warm for January, so I thought he was probably out getting a coffee or had walked down to his business establishment a few blocks away.

Without thinking much more about it, I returned to pick up Peg after her curling match and went back to my office. I called Shawn's place and left a message for him to call me. It was early in the evening, and, after calling again and receiving no answer, I felt a bit uneasy. However, I thought he might be out with one of his friends, so I didn't really get too anxious about it. Later that evening, I decided to go over to talk with him and took the spare apartment key he kept at our home so I could let myself in if he was still out. When I arrived, I noticed the truck was there and knocked at the door but got no response. I still felt he was probably out with his friends. However, as I put the key in the door, I had a terrible sense of foreboding that I could not explain. I opened the door and saw him lying on the couch and knew immediately something terrible had happened. It was the most sickening feeling I have ever experienced. Instantly, I took in what had happened. My son had shot himself with my hunting rifle which I had not used for years and had kept locked in a cabinet in the basement of my house. I staggered and almost collapsed.

I stood there in shock, my mind trying to make some sense of what I was seeing. My senses were telling me one thing, but my mind could not accept it. It was the most horrible sight I have ever witnessed—so much so, it was very difficult to accept it as reality and not a terrible nightmare. I was beside myself, pacing around the room, raging, groaning, crying, not knowing what to do with myself. It was several minutes before I could pull myself together enough to call 911. Those few moments were the most terrible imaginable.

After making the call, I went outside to wait for the police and paramedics as I was asked to do. In a very few moments, the police arrived. The first officer on the scene asked me what had happened, and I briefly told him what I found. He was visibly troubled on learning who it was as he had worked with Shawn frequently when Shawn worked for the Sheriff's Office. He was very gracious and considerate with me and took care of such matters as calling the funeral home and facilitating the removal of Shawn's body. He asked me if he could take me home, but I told him I was able to drive myself.

Finding Shawn's body has been the most horrible event of my life. I cannot explain the horror and absolutely sickening feeling that resulted from discovering my son lying dead on his couch. That moment lies fixed in my memory and replays often, much to my dread. Still reliving that moment is one of the worst things I have to live with and is something I must accept as part of my continuing reality. I am very grateful to God that I was the one who found him rather than Peg, Neil or Jaclyn or one of Shawn's close friends. I would not want any of them to live with such a terrible memory. I can understand what Dale Byers and his family experienced on finding their dead son, a suicide victim, in the woods behind their home (Byers, 1991). The shock of finding a child dead from suicide creates a horrible nightmare that has no equal. The incredible finality and darkness of death is overwhelming and creates such a feeling of helplessness. As I stood viewing the body of my son, my heart cried out to do something, but there was nothing I could do. It was such a debilitating experience. I was never so conscious of my finite existence as at that time. I could do nothing but stand in horror and despair, crying to God and receiving no answer. The utter helplessness I felt completely devastated me.

Knowing I would need help in breaking the news to Peg, I stopped at Steve and Judy Dempster's so they could come with me. I was so grateful their house was on my way home. Steve is a wonderful colleague of mine at Atlantic Baptist University, and he and Judy are two of the most compassionate, empathetic and loving people I have ever known. I knew I would need such people to help me as I went home to tell Peg. I told them what I had found, and they immediately comforted me and agreed to follow me home. When I entered the house, Peg was in the family room on the couch. As I walked down the steps into the room, Peg seemed to know immediately something was wrong. I told her briefly what I had found, and we wept in each other's arms on the couch. The depth of pain and grief was almost unbearable as we agonized over the loss of our son. I'm so thankful Steve and Judy were there as they surrounded Peg and me with their love and support, held us, cried with us and empathized with our pain during the most terrible moments we have ever endured together.

It is amazing how you can still function even at such a time. Over the next few hours, we called family and friends to tell them what had happened. The first two calls were the most difficult I have ever made. I called Neil, Shawn's younger brother by two years. He was at a friend's house, and all I could say was that he should come home quickly as something terrible had happened. He arrived in a few minutes, and I shared with him what had happened. We held each other and cried and tried to comfort each other as best we could in the face of such a horrible incident. He stayed for a little while, then felt he needed to go tell Shawn's closest friends. As they were also his friends, I think he needed their support at that terrible time as well. The second call was to Jaclyn, Shawn's sister, seven years younger. Jaclyn was in Orlando, Florida working as an exchange student for a year with the Disney Corporation. I will always be very grateful for her wonderful friends in Orlando who cared for her in so many ways. Within a few minutes of receiving the news that her brother was dead (I did not give her the details of how it happened), her apartment was filled with people facilitating her return to Canada. Their loving assistance will always be remembered.

After calling a number of other family members and close friends, we went to bed to try to get a couple of hours of fitful sleep which we never really got. In the morning, Peg and I went to the funeral home to make the necessary arrangements. Nothing hammers home the reality of what has happened like picking out the coffin. It was dreadful, looking at coffins for our son, knowing his body was in a room close by. I cannot describe the despairing feeling in the pit of my stomach as we went through this necessary exercise. As I look back, it all seems like a daze, but we did what we had to do. Although I didn't feel very spiritual at the time, I was still aware of my relationship with God and that He promised to be with us even in such a situation as we were experiencing. That knowledge was a source of strength during those terrible moments.

I am still profoundly grateful for the loving response during the visiting hours on Saturday and the funeral on Sunday afternoon. People came by the hundreds and the outpouring of affirmation, love, support and caring is something I will never forget. The fact that so many people made a point of sharing with us in our hour of need has left an indelible impression on me. God's provision for us through His people was marvelous. I have learned how important it is to come alongside people in their pain. We don't have to have the right answers or the most profound words, just our loving presence is usually enough. A tear, a hug, a hand on the shoulder speak volumes. Many of those wonderful people will probably never know how meaningful their supporting presence was to us during that terrible crisis.

An unexpected situation for me was the inability of other members of the family to experience a sense of closure with Shawn. Because of how he died, he was in a closed casket, and saying goodbye to his visible presence was not possible for them. I realized this when, on Saturday evening, I heard my daughter, Jaclyn, ask the funeral director if she could have the casket opened to view his body. She explained to me that she could not convince her mind he was really dead in that coffin. Since I was the only family member to actually see his body, I realized their reality of his death was quite different from mine. We agreed that, although she could not view the entire body, we could come back after visiting hours and they would arrange to have some of the body exposed so she could have a sense of closure. Jaclyn, myself and a very close, life-long friend, Mike Kaye went back to the funeral home that evening, and Jaclyn was able to experience the physical reality of her brother's body. She touched his arms and chest, caressing as much as was exposed. The next day, Peg and I went back early so Peg could also view her son and thus have some assistance in accepting the reality of what had happened. She also needed to touch and caress her son for the last time on this earth. I'm not sure why it was a need for Jaclyn and Peg to actually touch him as I never felt this need. Perhaps it has something to do with how we socialize females in our society to be more sensitive to touch. It did help them in coping with what had happened and in saying a final goodbye.

I have two major reasons for writing this account. First, I hope it will help my family and me cope with what has happened and prove therapeutic for us as we work through the incredible shock of Shawn's death. The process towards wholeness is a long and difficult one, and systematically examining the events that have rocked our family more than we could have imagined can be part of our healing. We may not find all the answers we are looking for, but it will be helpful to at least ask the questions.

Secondly, I sincerely pray that the story of our situation, both the struggles and victories, may be of some assistance to others who are also coping with tremendous loss and pain. We have found encouragement, strength, comfort and helpful information from the accounts of others who have shared their healing journey. Perhaps we can do the same through this account.

Chapter 1

Who Was Shawn?

TO HELP the reader more fully relate to this account, I first want to introduce the person who is the central figure in what has happened so you can experience, in even a small way, a sense of who he was and get a glimpse of the reality of this young man. Born on April 9, 1971, Shawn was eagerly anticipated and such a source of joy when he arrived into this world. After three years of married life, Peg and I looked forward to our new roles as parents. A few months after Shawn's birth, we moved from Fredericton, New Brunswick where I worked as an economist for the N.B. government, to Moncton, N.B. to commence my teaching career at Atlantic Baptist University. Peg, a Bachelor of Nursing graduate of the University of New Brunswick, also commenced a new job as director of a nursing research project at the Moncton Hospital. We lived almost across the street from my parents, so my mother, a wonderful woman who loved children, looked after

Shawn during the day, and Peg and I cared for him in the evenings and weekends. Having such a loving, secure environment his first couple of years of life had a profound impact on his personality development. He grew up with a gentle, loving spirit, secure in who he was. He was a very good student all through school. In high school, he was a principal's list student each year, played varsity basketball, football and captained the school rugby team. He also tutored special-needs students and had a wonderful way with those who struggled with life because of physical or mental impairments. He accepted them just as they were and treated them as valued people. They responded to him with loving affection. I remember meeting the teacher who supervised the special needs students at the high school and mentioned I was Shawn's father. Her faced lit up, and she laughingly stated, "Oh yes, the young man with the muscles." Shawn also worked out in the weight room to help him with his other sports activities. She told me she was so impressed with Shawn's gentleness with the students he tutored.

While attending Atlantic Baptist University, he captained the varsity basketball team, chaired the sports committee and, in his senior year, was a Resident Assistant, a key student leadership position at the university. I remember what an incredible delight it was for me to have Shawn attending the school at which I taught. He was a constant source of joy and pride. He graduated with the highest academic standing in the graduating class and received a full academic scholarship to Acadia University's Master of Arts program in Wolfville, Nova Scotia.

Much more significant than any of those accomplishments was his decision to commit his life to the Lord. While just a young boy of ten, he asked Jesus into his life. After drifting somewhat from the faith in high school, he rededicated his life to the Lord late one night in the ABU residence. I remember getting the phone call at 2:00 a.m. and feeling such a sense of dread when the phone rang. As the University's Dean of Campus Life, responsible for the residences among other things, I knew my phone only rang that late when it was bad news. This was so wonderfully different. It was Shawn, calling to tell me of his decision and saying he wanted me to be the first to know. It was one of the most wonderful moments of my entire life. From my own experience, I can believe the statement that our children give us our best and worst moments. That phone call provided one of my best. Shawn's subsequent baptism at Hillside Baptist Church in Moncton and his public testimony before the church are wonderful highlights of my life that still provide me with comfort as I know he is now with his Lord. Without that assurance, life would be almost unbearable. The hope of the resurrection, the assurance that we will meet again and that this life is just the forerunner to life in glory, have become so much more meaningful. It enables us to live in hope rather than just exist in despair.

After graduating from ABU, Shawn spent two years at Acadia University where he graduated with his Master of Arts degree in sociology. The summer he was at Acadia, the movie *Dolores Claiborne* was being made in Nova Scotia with part of it filmed in Wolfville. It was quite an experience for him as he was a bit of a movie buff, and he got a job working on the movie set. Two of his prized possessions from the summer were a cap given to him by one of the stunt men—which I still have—and a copy of Stephen King's book autographed by Cathy Bates, the star of the movie.

He returned to Moncton after finishing his degree and worked at odd jobs for a year or so. One of his jobs was working with handicapped children in Moncton's group homes. He was so good with them, and they loved him. He then got a job with the Sheriff's Office and worked there until the fall of 1998 when he left to establish his own business, a small retail outlet in downtown Moncton. He was somewhat frustrated at not being able to get a job that utilized his qualifications but seemed very excited to be setting up his own store. He had expressed a desire to launch out on his own and had planned for this business venture for over a year. He knew it was a temporary venture and indicated that probably, after a couple of years, he would go back to school to continue his training.

During all this time, he frequently dropped by our home even though he was living with a couple of his closest friends. In fact, we had almost daily contact. In the spring of 1998, he took a couple months leave from the Sheriff's Office to tour Europe. It had been a dream of his for a long time and proved to be a tremendous time for him as he experienced so many different places and people. He called regularly, and, when he returned, he shared his pictures of the trip. As there was no one who could go with him, he planned and completed the trip by himself, traveling through England, Scotland, France, Spain, Italy, Hungary, Germany and Holland. I expressed to him my admiration at his courage and competence as I doubt if I would even consider doing such a thing myself.

It was his loving and gentle personality that so endeared him to all who knew him. He was generous to a fault, and our home has many reminders of his giving nature including the stand our TV sits on, a magazine holder (both Christmas gifts) and a limited print of golfer Lee Trevino which he brought back from Europe for me as he knew I was an avid golfer. I prize this highly, and it now hangs in my office. He also brought back jewelry and other gifts from Europe for Peg, Jaclyn and Neil. They are constant reminders of who he was. For example, the gold earrings he brought back for Jaclyn are her favouritess. He found a real joy in sharing what he had with others. It is so hard to comprehend that this wonderful young man, loved dearly by so many, chose to leave this life. It is a reality we find very difficult to understand or accept.

Mike Kaye, one of my closest and dearest friends since child-hood whose wife, Joyce, is Peg's best friend, gave the eulogy at the funeral and expressed some of the essence of who Shawn was. He said:

> As I thought about Shawn over the years he was with us, and as I listened to many of the comments of his family and his friends, the word "*good*" was used again and again. "He was a *good* guy!"... He loved deeply and without reserve. One of his rugby buddies said, "He had a *good* heart"—a gentle heart.
>
> It was a *good* heart that was filled with compassion for anyone who needed him. He bore their burdens.... He was a *good* friend....
>
> One thing that has struck me the most about Shawn is his relationship with Neil and Jaclyn.... "He was a *good* brother," Neil said. "He was the nicest guy I ever knew."... He was a *good* big brother to Jaclyn. Shawn was that listening ear when Jaclyn needed someone older and wiser....
>
> Shawn was a *good* leader. He led by example whether he was in the workplace, at school, with the team, or at home....
>
> Shawn was a *good* son to Peggy and Gary, a joy in their lives....
>
> Shawn had a *good* faith. He loved his heavenly Father.... He would agree that any goodness in him was because of Christ living within....
>
> Let us incorporate Shawn's *goodness* and the qualities of his life that we celebrate into our own lives so that his influence and memory will live on in us... that this "*good guy*" can, through us, love and touch others as he has touched our lives.
>
> Shawn, you left us too soon! We will miss you! We love you!

Chapter 2

Surviving
the Initial Days

AS A GRIEVING family, we have experienced two phases in coping with this terrible event. The first phase involved just making it through each new day as it dawned. Surviving each hour, with the pain and grief, was all we could handle. Contemplating the longer-term perspective was beyond our ability. But as days passed into weeks, we were able to facilitate a process that could enable more protracted healing to occur. This chapter will outline some of the factors involved in surviving those initial days. Subsequent chapters will relate how more long-term healing took place in our lives.

Our initial reaction to Shawn's untimely death was overwhelming grief and shock. Throughout the weekend, a numbing emptiness pervaded our lives as we went through the motions of the visiting hours and the funeral. It was like we were in another world yet also aware of the actual one and still able to function within it, doing what had to be done. It was a strangeness such as I had never experienced before. It is as if the body and mind numbs itself to the terrible pain so that the person continues to function.

The visiting hours on Saturday and the funeral on Sunday afternoon, as difficult as they were to experience, were also very therapeutic for us. The outpouring of love, sympathy and practical help was beyond anything we could have expected. Close friends and family came to our home to comfort and support. People arrived by the hundreds to express their condolences to us, some traveling from fairly distant places. The funeral, so meaningfully handled by the pastoral staff of our home church, Hillside Baptist, and Mike's eulogy, were an incredible tribute to Shawn and how his relatively short life of twenty-seven years had still positively touched many people. The way so many wonderful people put their loving arms around us in our time of need is something we cherish dearly and will never forget. The funeral home was filled far beyond its capacity, and the patience and graciousness demonstrated by so many people touched us very deeply. The entire Moncton rugby team, on which Shawn had played, came as a group to the funeral. It was a marvelous tribute to Shawn by these caring young men.

The weekend drew our family very close together as we shared our pain and tried to comfort and strengthen each other. The composure and strength of both Neil and Jaclyn were such blessings to me as their inner strength of character shown through in such a terrible situation. I had feared for Neil as he had lost his best friend in an automobile accident the summer after his first year in university, and I did not know what this further traumatic blow would do to him.

Pain and Loss

Monday came, and the crowds were gone. The funeral was over, and we were left with our thoughts and grief. Extended family members and close friends maintained frequent contact and helped us handle those first few days and weeks. But Shawn was still gone. Some of the numbness had gone, but I had such an emptiness inside and experienced such intense pain it was almost unbearable. It was the worst anguish imaginable. I sobbed and groaned for the son I would never see again in this life. I missed his presence so much, the thought of never having him around was excruciating. I felt I had not just lost a son, but part of me was gone and would never return. Parental grief over the loss of a child involves not only grieving for the child who is gone but for the loss of part of oneself. We have lost a person we were responsible for bringing into the world, someone who originated in ourselves and represented an attachment bond like none other.

Therefore, the intensity of the pain those first few weeks was directly related to this unique and deep sense of loss experienced. As Shawn was such an integral and wonderful part of our lives, it was almost incomprehensible for us to imagine life without him. The fact that life will never be the same is not easy to accept as it also means accepting that the pain is real and will never fully go away. As long as we have memory, the pain of Shawn's death will never fully abate. We have lost part of ourselves, and there will be a "hole in our hearts" for the rest of our lives.

Physical Manifestations of Grief

In addition to the terrible sense of emotional loss we experienced with Shawn's death, there were physical manifestations of grief which I naively had not expected and for which I was not prepared. I have known for a long time that emotional turmoil can take its toll physically and that many real physical symptoms, like headaches, stomach trouble, and chest pains, can have an emotional source. But to have it impact myself at such a level was another story.

Both Peg and I were literally sick to our stomachs for weeks after his death. It was a horrible feeling that was constantly there and from which there was no relief. It lasted for about three weeks before finally subsiding. Jaclyn shared with us that, after receiving the news in Orlando, she was sick to her stomach, experienced vomiting and shook all over for hours. She wondered if she would be able to fly home. Neil shared with me that Paul Scharnberg, Shawn's closest friend, had such severe pains in his chest when told the news he thought he might be having a heart attack. It has been a reminder to me of how our bodies, although made up of many parts, are whole systems, and something that affects one part will have ramifications for the other parts. Such an emotional blow spread to the physical realm, and we suffered on a number of levels. I believe this is one of the things that makes grieving such a dreadful experience. It affects our whole being, permeating every aspect of our existence.

Anger

Anger is usually expected when a parent loses a child as anger is the most ready emotion we experience when deprived of something we value and love. We may be angry at the departed one for leaving, at God for allowing it to happen or anyone else in the vicinity, even ourselves. This would seem especially true in the case of suicide. When a loss is so unnatural and unexpected, anger at what has happened is not unusual. Iris Bolton, whose twenty-year-old son committed suicide, states:

> I felt rage, violent and consuming. I was angry at God, then at myself, and eventually at my son. Sometimes I even felt guilty because I was so angry at my beloved child. A sense of inescapable injustice haunted me (Bolton, 1986:204).

However, in the days that followed Shawn's death, I was amazed at the complete absence of anger towards Shawn in Peg and I. It was rather unexpected as most of the literature dealing with suicide says it is inevitable. Jaclyn, however, in her deep anguish, expressed anger, through her tears, the first night after she arrived home. But on Sunday evening, as we talked together, trying to make some sense of what had happened, Shawn's loving nature and the fact that he would never deliberately hurt anyone was expressed by all of us so clearly. It really left no room for anger except at the terrible waste of a promising young life. Anger towards Shawn has not been an issue, even three-and-a-half years later.

James and Friedman, in *The Grief Recovery Handbook* (1998), do question the assumption that anger is always a factor in loss. They express that the circumstances, not just the death, may be an important factor in the presence or absence of anger.

For us, our grief, rather than surfacing lingering anger at Shawn, has evoked a deep compassion towards him as the inner turmoil he was suffering must have been dreadful for him to even attempt such an action. For myself, rather than feeling anger, I hurt for the pain he must have been experiencing, and I regret I was not aware of how deep it was. Shawn thought his death would solve problems and erase his hurt. The personal hurt he was experiencing may be gone, but the additional hurt and pain created by his death has been incalculable. As Dale Byers (Byers, 1991) notes, the hurt is multiplied by each family member, each friend, by all the people who knew and loved him. I guess, in the end, I am only angry with myself and the circumstances involved in such a tragedy. I am so thankful that anger towards Shawn has not been a continuing companion of our family as the other painful emotions are enough to handle.

Lack of Understanding

Since the very first day, we have not been able to make any sense of Shawn's death, and that has plagued us every day. Not knowing the reasons for something is much harder for me than knowing even a very hurtful reason. At least knowing some reason, even a very terrible one, allows for some sense of closure and finality in one's mind. But that has not been true in Shawn's case. Although he was struggling with many of the same things we all struggle with in this fallen world—disappointment, some unrealized expectations, modern day stress and so on—there was nothing we detected in his daily activities that would have helped us predict what happened. Logically thinking, given his family, friends and his faith, suicide should never have been an option. But it was, and there lies the dilemma.

I will never forget sitting in our living room a couple days after the funeral with Shawn's best friends, guys he had known most of his life, strong, powerful yet gentle rugby buddies with whom he had shared a house. I listened to these hurting men express, through their sobs, consternation at this terrible event they just could not understand. "He must have known how much he was loved," they cried in their frustration and grief. It just made no sense.

Later, I expressed to Neil my struggle with trying to make sense of this and he said, "Dad, there was no logical reason for what happened to Shawn. He was not experiencing any unusual pressures that we all have not experienced. It must have been something else we cannot explain at this time."

Was it because of environmental pressures? Was there a genetic disposition? Was it a combination of factors that caused him such despair that evening? My daughter, Jaclyn, once shared with me that, even with an external environment characterized by love and accomplishments, one may feel an internal emptiness "that consumes your every happiness and all the love that surrounds you, leaving you inexplicably sad and so lonely, feeling starved for joy." We may never know for sure what actually happened and why. That has made our lives very difficult. It has been an important factor in the spiritual struggles that emerged shortly after Shawn's death.

Spiritual Struggles

In the first few weeks, probably one of the most difficult struggles we had to endure was on the spiritual level. Not only was Shawn the product of a loving environment which he often acknowledged, but he was a committed Christian. How could this happen given these variables? I have pondered deep and long, almost to the point of despair, attempting to find some kind of answer. So far, I have been unsuccessful in answering many of my questions and am finally accepting the fact that I will never, in my life, fully understand what happened.

I have found, as I reflect back, that I went through a three-stage process in my spiritual struggles. Initially, my cry was, "Where is God? How could this happen to His child?" I was confronted with a terrible silence. As in Job's case, I received no answer from God initially. It seemed God was absent at our most needful time. The feelings of abandonment were overwhelming. Like the writer of Psalms, I cried out, "Why, O LORD, do you stand far off? Why do you hide yourself in times of trouble?" (Psalm 10:1). I questioned the goodness of God, His care for us, and pondered, like C.S. Lewis, that I would not be in danger of ceasing to believe in God but that I might believe He is something He is not—that God really is not concerned with us at all (Lewis, 1961).

However, I gradually realized God was not absent, and He was ministering to us in many ways, primarily through His people. He had not forsaken us, and we had His strength and comfort as each day required. I was drawn back to His Book and to prayer as I had not been before. I realized that I was dependent on Him for power to endure what was happening. And, while I found tremendous encouragement and solace from my drawing back to the Lord, I also was confronted with the God of the Bible who, in many ways, differed from our cultural stereotypes. It moved me to the third stage in my spiritual journey. I began to reevaluate my whole view of who God is, what He allows and why He does not prevent such pain in His children. I poured over such books as *Disappointment with God* and *The Jesus I Never Knew* by Philip Yancey, *Knowing God* by J.I. Packer, Charles Swindoll's *The Quest for Character*, R.C. Sproul's *Reason to Believe*, Charles Colson's *How Now Shall We Live*, C.S. Lewis' *A Grief Observed*. I also reviewed Bill Bright's series on the *Characteristics of God* and perused many other references that have had a profound effect on my perceptions of who our God really is. This has been a very significant part of my healing journey.

Rescue Fantasies

As I wrestled with my feelings about what had happened, I was constantly reviewing in my mind how I could have prevented Shawn's suicide. For the first few weeks, I fantasized over and over again how I could have prevented Shawn's action. These rescue fantasies have continued for a long time. I have pictured myself arriving at his apartment before the event and working it out with him. I imagined us talking about how he felt and together resolving his difficulties. In my mind, I have rehearsed advice I could have given him to help him handle life more effectively. I have thought of ways I could have helped him spiritually, to better trust and rely on God. Even though I realize these fantasies are in the context of what has already happened and not the context of the world we were in before Shawn's death, they still replay occasionally even yet. They are not as frequent as before but, every now and then when his loss overwhelms me and I miss him so much, my mind explores ways I could have helped him still be here. Even now, I have moments when I cannot believe he is gone. It seems so unbelievable. I picture him coming in the front door, standing in my office, walking down the halls of ABU, sitting in the family room, and the fact that he is really gone just cannot register in my mind. It seems that, confronted with so much pain, the mind seeks to relieve the anguish by attempting to reverse the past, to mentally find ways to make it as if it never happened. Unfortunately, manufactured mental images cannot undue what has been done, and the reality of the actual events eventually overpowers all our fantasies.

Heart vs. Head Struggles

Therefore, much of what I experienced in those early days after Shawn's death played out as a heart vs. head struggle. The head realized what had happened, knew the facts of the case, could logically relate what had happened, but my heart could not accept it. It wanted nothing to do with logic. It wanted Shawn back and the pain to cease. I found I was in intellectual acceptance but emotional denial. Relating to this, I found in literature some confusion about the concept of denial. By denial, I don't mean I was not cognitively aware that Shawn had died, but rather that my heart had real trouble accepting it had happened. My head knows he is dead, but it stretches the limits of credibility of what my heart can accept. There are days even now when I feel disbelief at what happened, experience shock, and my heart cannot accept that such a thing could happen. But a few minutes later, I can calmly accept Shawn's death as a reality I cognitively acknowledge. Later, I may be overwhelmed by feelings of helplessness and despair. The struggle is not as overwhelming now as before, but, from my experience, it does continue for some time. Part of the healing process may well be a diminishing of this struggle as the heart learns over time to better cope with what has happened and, consequently, the pain becomes less acute.

Helplessness

One of the most horrible feelings I experienced as I looked upon Shawn's body was the debilitating sense of helplessness that overwhelmed me like a black cloud. I believe being impacted so severely by events over which one cannot exercise any control is one of the major issues all grieving parents, friends and family members have to handle. It is so exasperating to hurt so deeply, to feel such a tremendous sense of loss and pain and not be able to do anything about it. To accept it is out of our hands probably is an important step to recovery, but it is not an easy step, especially for a problem-solver like myself who has always wanted to protect and fix everything for my family. This I could not fix, and I paced the floor in frustration many nights asking God to calm my heart and help me accept that which I could not change.

As the studies tell us time and time again, males in our society are culturally trained to be problem-solvers, to take charge of situations that effect us, to stand stoically in the face of adversity. Therefore, to be face-to-face with a situation over which I had absolutely no control was devastating. To this day, recalling those dreadful moments sometimes triggers intense feelings of hopelessness and anxiety. I have learned that the impact of such things internalizes on our deepest levels and is not easily overcome. The good news is that, while it may not be easy to overcome, it is not impossible. I am much better now at giving over to the Lord that which I cannot control. My helplessness is compensated by His sufficiency.

Fear

In the weeks and months that followed Shawn's death, I realized I had a heightened fear for my other children, almost to the point of panic. If I came home and there was no one there, my anxiety increased remarkably, and I fretted about where everyone was and what they might be doing. I slowly realized that what I really feared was that Neil or Jaclyn might take the same action that had claimed Shawn's life. It was a horrible feeling that pervaded my being constantly. I was never free of it. I know that when one is in an accident or some other calamity, the fear of another one increases. For example, if one of our children has a car accident, we worry more the next time they take the car. However, I found this trepidation for other family members was quite different from any apprehension I had experienced in other contexts. The fear that you could lose another child to suicide is a sickening, debilitating feeling that I struggled with for some time. Although, as a family, we had talked about how Shawn's decision must never be an option for anyone else, I finally had to talk about my fears to Peg, Neil and Jaclyn. Believing part of the context of Shawn's death may have been a biological predisposition increased my fear, since my other children have similar genetic make-ups.

As we shared with each other about how we felt, the fears we carried and the options available if we had suicidal tendencies, my fears subsided. Opening these issues with the children and outlining strategies to handle such eventualities was comforting. We agreed that, if we ever felt such compulsions, we would talk with one another before any action was taken. We contracted together to be each other's lifeline. I pray every day that, if any other member of my family ever feels as Shawn must have been feeling, they will immediately contact me or someone else who can help them through such a time. I am so conscious that a call to a parent, friend, pastor or the local suicide hotline number could save a life.

The Lord has been gracious as I have confronted this fear in my life. I have been reminded again that, as Christians, we are not to have the spirit of fear. His Word teaches us that He has not given us the spirit of fear, but, as 1 John reminds us, His perfect love drives out fear. We still have the responsibility to do anything helpful to handle fear, but He promises to bless our efforts and provide His presence so that living in fear ceases to be our daily reality.

I also feared how people might interpret Shawn's action and the discouragement and disillusionment his death might cause others who knew him, especially non-Christian friends. Would Shawn's faith be nullified in their eyes because of what he had done? Would our Christian witness as a family be compromised because of the action of a member? Most of my fears were unfounded as people displayed a level of compassion and empathy that were sources of great comfort to me. Although everyone found it very difficult to understand, they did not hesitate to give Shawn the benefit of the doubt for something that made no sense to any of us. The loving reaction of people, the opposite of a condemning attitude, has been such a blessing to us.

Guilt

Guilt is the feeling that we have done something wrong, have failed to meet expectations or have violated a standard, and it is a common feeling for us humans. It is especially prevalent in parents as we never seem to reach that plateau of perfection in child rearing that we expect of ourselves and feel everyone else expects. Because of this, guilt is often a dominating presence when a child dies. Therefore, when the death of a child occurs for any reason, we second-guess ourselves almost to distraction. I believe this is the case regardless of how the death occurred. For example, if the child dies because of sickness, we blame ourselves for not doing enough to facilitate their healing, or we fear we did not do enough to prevent the disease in the first place, or we may blame ourselves for somehow transmitting the disease to the child. In the case of an accident, we play over and over in our minds what we could have done to prevent what happened: if only we had not given the child the car, if only we had driven more carefully, if only we had instructed the child more thoroughly, and on it goes. In most cases, the truth is that we did all we could and had very little control over the actual event that took the life of our child. We cannot see the future and must act as best we can in the present. Only hindsight is twenty-twenty when it comes to evaluating disasters. We know this in our heads. But it takes some time for this reality to take root in out hearts so we can stop blaming ourselves for what happened. We tend to be hardest on ourselves, and self-condemnation can hinder the healing process as we struggle with the loss.

I am constantly reminded of how quickly disaster can strike, even with the best precautions. We live in an uncertain world where rain falls on both the godly and ungodly. Wonderful things happen to most of us, and tragedy befalls most of us as well. God does not grant His people immunity from disaster. What He does provide is the comfort and strength to endure the misfortune. I was vividly reminded of this as my wife and I traveled south from Moncton, N.B., Canada to commence a month's sabbatical/vacation in South Carolina where I could work on this manuscript. We were only three hours from our home when, as we were driving along the highway, an elderly gentleman pulled right out in front of us, attempting to cross the highway from a rest stop. He did not see us at all, and before we could react, the front of our car smashed into the side of his truck. It all happened in a split second, and the front end of our car was reduced to a tangled mess. The air bags deployed, and miraculously, we were left relatively unscathed. But I realized that, in a split second, even with the best defensive driving possible, both my wife and I could have been ushered into eternity. We live in a world where these events happen every moment, and there is little that we can do about that fact. We have to do our best and leave the rest to a sovereign God.

In the case of suicide, the process of coping with the guilt seems much more complex and prolonged. If our child decides to take his/her life, what does that say about us as parents and how we related to that child? Arnaldo Pangrazzi states:

> You may feel that somehow you did not love enough, or that your relationship was not good enough. You keep rehearsing all the "if onlys": "Why didn't I realize how sick he was?" "If only I had been home on time" (Pangrazzi, 1988).

The feeling that you could somehow have prevented this is overwhelming, and the blame and guilt are almost unbearable.

I still second-guess the car accident and wonder if I could have seen the truck a bit sooner, if I could have anticipated that he would not see us, etc. But that is nothing compared to what I experienced with Shawn's death. I have agonized over how he could do such a thing and I not see any indication that he was contemplating such a move. I have "if only-ed" myself to distraction. If only I had gone to his apartment first rather than my doctor's appointment. If only I had left my office just a few minutes earlier and arrived home while he was still there. If only I had been more sensitive to his moods, etc. If only I had not been so preoccupied with my own cancer diagnosis and been more attuned to Shawn's life. If only I had realized how devastating the news of my cancer was to Shawn. If only I had been more involved in his business activity. Even though I know intellectually I did the best I could given the circumstances, and that life was no rougher or smoother for us than most other families, my heart still has trouble accepting what has happened and feels that somehow I could have done more to prevent it. The struggle between the heart and head continues. Part of the resolution of that struggle is to finally realize we cannot judge what happened yesterday by what we know today.

Work

In the first few weeks after Shawn's death, I remember just going through the motions with very little incentive or motivation to do anything. As I look back, I am amazed I was able to teach my classes, go to the University, interact with faculty, staff and students. I admit much of the time my head was in a daze. Activity, however, is a way I am able to cope with difficulties, and returning to work was very beneficial for me. Some thought I was being very courageous and was handling Shawn's death so well, but the truth is, I was going through my usual routines as a way to survive the terrible pain I was experiencing. Conducting my classes, sharing with faculty and staff and working in my office allowed the pain to be deflected somewhat and prevented my mind from being completely preoccupied with the terrible internal trauma I was experiencing. I will be forever grateful to the wonderful people at ABU who so lovingly cared for me, probably without consciously knowing what a tremendous help they were being to me.

My primary area of academic study is family sociology, and one of my favourite courses is that particular one: Marriage and Family. I have taught for years about the variables involved in family crises, the impact of the loss of family members, the process individuals go through in recovery and so on. I was one month into my Marriage and Family course when Shawn died. What a different experience it was for both me and the class. As we reviewed how the death of a child creates the highest stress level in a family, as we discussed the grief process and what individuals experience when families are impacted by death, as we studied what is required for healing, as we looked at the role of Christian faith in handling death, I was not an impartial observer sharing with the class what the studies had indicated. I was experiencing in my own life and family much of what we were reviewing.

Many times I was unable to teach without my voice breaking and tears coming to my eyes. But I was able to share my feelings with the class, and some of them, who had also experienced painful losses, were also able to share. I don't know if the academic content was as extensive as it was in other years, but the emotional content and the actual learning that took place in that class was probably greater than had ever taken place before. The academic component and the experiential came together as never before. We learned about the process, but we also learned much about each other and how to sensitively interact with each other in times of pain. The students' compassion and empathy for me was wonderful and contributed more to my personal healing than they will ever know.

To a certain extent, my work gave me a forum in which I could express, at least in part, what was happening in my life, especially with colleagues. In addition, the class setting also gave opportunities to share less specifically when appropriate and gave a sense of authenticity, both to me and the material being reviewed. However, I am not suggesting that this course of action is appropriate for everyone as part of their individual healing process. A "go right back to work" proposal may be terrible advice for many who may need space from their employment to aid their recovery process. Although, because of my particular personality and work environment, it was very helpful for me to continue with my vocation, it may not work for someone else whose personality and/or work environment may not be conducive to such an early return.

Necessary Tasks

One of the harsh realities we must face during a personal or family crisis is that the rest of the world continues on as usual. We may wish the world would stop while we struggle with our personal trauma, but it doesn't. Therefore, we have to handle all the necessary tasks involved in living even when we are just attempting to personally survive. Some tasks (related to the crisis or otherwise) just can't wait until we feel strong enough to cope with such duties. For example, in the case of a death, funeral arrangements must be made. Thank goodness for the help and graciousness of those involved, such as the funeral home staff and the pastoral staff at Hillside who facilitated so well this painful task.

In the days that followed, there were so many other tasks that had to be attended to for which I had very little strength or motivation to handle. The most difficult was wrapping up Shawn's business venture. Going through his papers, contracts, etc., many of which we had jointly compiled, was heart-wrenching. As I examined his notes, his progress reports, his time schedules, and so on, there were times when I would just collapse in pangs of grief and anguish, sobbing uncontrollably. But somehow, it all got done as I talked to his suppliers, landlords, government agencies, etc. As I look back now, I am amazed at the strength we have to do such things when it is needed. While the tasks that must be accomplished differ with each situation, the fact of necessary tasks is common to all. The hardest to do are those that involve the one departed. With so much to do in those early days and weeks after his death that reminded me of Shawn, I was constantly confronted with the pain of separation from my son. Many of the things I had to do were a reinforcement of the grief I was experiencing. However, they did get done, and in the process, I probably became stronger as each was accomplished. I realized I could take care of what had to be done and survive the process as God gave me strength when needed.

While some tasks must be done right away, there are others that can wait until we feel strong enough to tackle them. Timing may be important as we deal with those necessary tasks, especially some directly related to the one we have lost. For example, sooner or later we have to decide what to do with the belongings of the one now gone. For most of us, it is a dreaded but necessary task. Timing here may be important, and how we accomplish this painful job may indicate how well we are handling the grieving process. At one extreme, we may immediately commence the disposal of the loved one's possessions before we have had time to think, grieve, recover from the shock, or before the reality of the situation has really had an impact on us. In this case, our disposal activity is probably a mechanism that helps us suppress the pain and anguish and prolong the denial stage. And unfortunately, we may do things and dispose of items we will later regret. On the other hand, we may avoid this activity altogether and make the departed loved one's area almost a shrine which will reinforce the pain over the long run and hinder any kind of adequate healing. Both extremes are counter-productive, as extremes are in most cases, and will block a healthy recovery.

If a healing process is under way, this difficult sorting and disposal undertaking can be part of that process. When you feel strong enough to handle this activity, knowing it will again pierce your heart with terrible anguish, that is the time to do it. For us, it was months after Shawn's death before we felt ready to go through his things and take the necessary actions. Jaclyn was back in Orlando and requested we only sort his clothes at this time as she wished to be involved in looking at his other possessions. It was a Saturday morning in May 1999 when Neil and I brought the boxes and bags that contained Shawn's belongings into the living room to sort them and decide what we would do with them. At this point, we were mainly looking at his clothes and everyday items he would have used as Jaclyn wanted to be present when we unpacked those more significant items that Shawn valued. We had already decided that what we could not use ourselves, we would give to the Head Start organization in Moncton for needy families.

I have to admit, I still was not prepared for the level of anguish that came over me as we sorted Shawn's things. It was almost as if we had just lost him, the pain was so severe. I was so grateful for Neil's presence as he gave me the strength I needed. Consequently, we had the composure to do what had to be done. What items we could use we kept, and the rest went to Head Start. Neil and Shawn were similar in size and traded clothes anyway, so what Neil felt he could use he put aside for himself, knowing Shawn would approve. I was able to do the same and still today have a special feeling when wearing something Shawn owned. However, Shawn's more prized possessions, for example, his valuable card collection, some antiques that he valued and other personal items, we left for Jaclyn's return. When she came back home from Florida, we completed the task. Neil wears with pride the beautiful watch Shawn had purchased in Europe, and Shawn's gold necklace, with the cross, is one of Jaclyn's most valued reminders of her brother. The other articles I stored in a trunk, or Peg and I have them in our home as warm reminders of Shawn. We tried to strike a balance between, on the one hand, disposing of any reminders as a way of ignoring the pain and loss and, on the other hand, keeping everything to avoid coping with what has really happened and suppressing the painful process necessary to cope with such a loss.

I found that handling such activities was important in illustrating to myself I could survive in a world which keeps going, even as mine had crashed. Those reserves of strength within us, and the help that comes from our Lord, carried us through those difficult early days.

Chapter 3

Learning to Live Again

TIME HAS a way of marching on. After the first few days and weeks had passed, when the paramount concern was survival, we now had to decide to commence a process of further healing that would enable us to bring back some sense of normality to our lives. We knew that the deeper the wound, the longer the healing process and the greater possibility that permanent damage may occur. And we had suffered a very deep wound. Even if healing goes well, lingering scar tissue may be a constant reminder of the damaging event. This is true for both physical and emotional wounding. The death of a child strikes the most devastating emotional blow we can receive. It cuts our hearts in two and brings our personal world crashing down. It is no wonder that, after the loss of a child, survival itself is usually our first concern. With such a devastating blow, we wonder if we will ever get back up. Getting on with our lives is not even in the equation initially.

Does that mean, however, that because we have suffered a loss that has changed our lives forever, recovery is not possible and we are destined to live the rest of our lives in misery and despair? Not at all. There were, however, some issues that needed some understanding and clarification as we attempted to facilitate our long-term healing.

"Getting Over" the Loss

There seems to be some confusion in the literature as to what is meant by "getting over" the loss. Part of the confusion comes from how we define what "getting over" means. The reaction to severe tragedy can range from permanent and debilitating emotional paralysis to seemingly full recovery with very little visible effects. James and Friedman state that:

> …one of the most damaging pieces of misinformation is the idea that you can "never get over" the death of a child. This absolutely incorrect claim is made to parents whose child has died…. There is a common and false picture created by grievers, by professionals, and by the literature: "Because I haven't forgotten her and still sometimes have feelings about her, I am not over the pain of the loss." This tragic setup is guaranteed to restrict and deflate the life of the griever (James and Friedman, 1998:15,16).

Given that our memories will remain intact, "getting over" our trauma must not be equated with "forgetting" what has happened and therefore defined as the absence of any lingering pain. If we are "complete" in our recovery when we no longer feel any pain at the remembrance of the loss, I guess, based on that criteria, I may never be complete. We need to be realistic at this point, and I personally believe a standard of "absence of pain" as the criteria for recovery sets up false expectations that may be very damaging to long-term healing. Both pain and joy are part of the human condition, and I am no more complete when I no longer feel pain than I would be if I could no longer feel joy. Some memories of Shawn bring a smile to my countenance while others bring a tear to my eye. "Getting over" Shawn does not mean reaching the point when tears are no longer possible. In fact, that I do not wish. As Iris Bolton, the mother of a son who committed suicide, so touchingly states:

> What a treasury of lessons your sacrifice has uncovered. Would that I never forget. And if I do... because I am human... let my scarred heart remind me gently with pangs of missing you (Bolton, 1986:211).

C.S. Lewis, in a moving little book, *A Grief Observed,* where he expresses his grief over the death of his wife, compares it to a man who has lost his leg. The stump will heal and the terrible pain will be over. He will "get over it." But he will only have one leg, which will change him forever. All the things that once were done, that the man took for granted, can no longer be accomplished. Even with an artificial leg, the man will never have two whole legs again. His life will never be the same (Lewis, 1961:43).

As a family, we will "get over" Shawn's death by learning to cope with both the joys and pain of his memory. The excruciating pain is mostly over, but lingering pangs will always be there as we reflect on his death. We must not see recovery as the absence of any sadness or pain. That is not "recovery" but more the stifling of emotions to cope with the pain. And if I stifle sadness, might I not also stifle joy? If my goal is to deaden those negative feelings, I may end up not being able to feel at all. If fact, much healing takes place when we can use our pain to reach out to others. Pangrazzi says it so well:

> You can choose to let your brokenness defeat you, or you can decide to get up and get going. Once you have the courage to place your hurt, your sensitivity, and your compassion at

the service of others, you have discovered the key to help yourself. For when pain is used to reach out to others, it becomes creative and transforming love (Pangrazzi, 1988:7).

"Getting over" our tragedy required a decision to survive and embrace life again. Most victims of terrible situations survive. How they survive is determined by their choices. As a family, we decided that we would do everything in our power to facilitate healing in our lives and prevent this painful act from destroying us as individuals or as a family unit, realizing that while pain and sorrow are inevitable, misery is optional. We have talked together, cried with each other, read articles /books that could help, prayed with and for each other, questioned what we did not understand, promoted hope for the future, laughed together and encouraged each other at every opportunity. It is getting better.

The Context of the Tragedy

The circumstances surrounding sudden loss and the context of the situation are crucial elements in the extent and depth of the subsequent grief response. The expected death of an elderly person will not surface the same response as the sudden shock of the unexpected death of a child. The context is obviously important when evaluating grief and loss. A very crucial variable in the level of grief and pain experienced when a loved one dies, and an important factor in emotional healing, is the nature of the relationship that existed with the departed one. The closer the relationship, the deeper will be the sense of loss with the passing of that loved one. If the relationship has been somewhat strained and distant, the sense of loss may not be as keenly felt although guilt and remorse may be heightened. The more intimate, the more rewarding, the more interactive, the more loving the relationship has been, the deeper will be the experience of the loss of their presence. We miss most what we value most, and we value most what we love and cherish most. Shawn was such a constant part of our lives and such a positive aspect of each day that his passing created a tremendous void that was immediately apparent. The joy of his daily visits to our home, my delight when he dropped by my office, his frequent demonstrations of his generous nature were part of our natural routine. His death cut away such a large part of our lives that full recovery, at least as defined by the absence of pain, will never be accomplished. My cancer operation, while eliminating the cancer, has also altered my body permanently although wonderful healing has taken place. Healing and recovery does not mean things are as they were before. The loss of Shawn has permanently altered our existence, and we will never be the same, either as individuals or as a family. With Shawn's death, we have lost part of ourselves. Rando points out the obvious but crucial factor that makes the loss of a child so painful. A child is the product of the parents and represents so much more to the parents than just another human being (Rando, 1986:7-10). Thus, the loss cuts deeper than any other tragedy. Bolton quotes the father of a sixteen-year-old who took her own life, saying: "Suicide is not a solitary act. A beloved person thinks she is killing only herself, but she also kills a part of us" (Bolton, 1986:202). Such a precious part of our lives, when gone, creates a permanent void.

The Reality of Separation

When someone precious and close has been lost, the awareness of that loss is very keen. There is a constant, nagging consciousness that the person's presence is no longer here. That in turn leads to a feeling of sadness. Therefore, the greater the awareness, the greater the sense of loss and consequently, the greater the feelings of grief and sadness.

Shawn was both a constant presence and a wonderful one. He

was a person we loved having around, and his loss is very deeply felt. I have found that, even three-and-a-half years later, something will remind me of Shawn, and the awareness of his absence still overwhelms me with a deep sense of loss, always accompanied with a profound sense of separation and a feeling of sadness. It can happen several times a day. It may be triggered by something I see—and there are scores of sights reminiscent of Shawn—or something I hear or something I am doing. I remember one day Peg and I were driving from the downtown area of Moncton to our home. The radio was on, and a song started playing that had been very popular at the time of Shawn's death. It triggered such a wave of grief and sadness I could hardly drive as the tears started to flow. There have been numerous times when tears have come because of some recollection, memory, article, etc.

Tears are one language God really understands. Tears are not a sign of weakness or lack of trust, but they indicate how deeply we have loved and therefore, how deeply we grieve. If it takes courage to love, tears illustrate we have had the courage to love deeply and now are experiencing the terrible pain of separation.

Consequently, I find there is still a constant sadness that is part of my everyday existence as I cope with the separation of my son. It is diminishing in its intensity as healing and recovery take place but still impacts my life by its presence. That does not mean I walk around melancholy and disconsolate, clouded in gloom and despair. I have my moments of joy and laughter. I have activities that give me pleasure and delight my heart. And, thank goodness, they are increasing. Despite that, there remains a prevailing, underlying sadness that surfaces easily, often and many times without any warning. Much of the zest for living has been diminished by the loss of Shawn. I fear it will never be fully recovered as the longing resulting from the loss of his presence will never completely subside.

Having said that, I am thankful that the inner joy of the Lord and the "peace that transcends circumstances" (Philippians 4:6–7) still abides in my life. By this, I don't mean "good feelings." Since Shawn's death, I have had many times when my life has been devoid of positive feelings, transplanted by grief and pain. At times, the joy of the Lord has nothing to do with good feelings and happiness. It is the knowledge that, as His children, He will never forsake us. It is the confidence of knowing that, in terrible situations, He has promised to provide the strength needed to survive. It is relying on a constant God, rather than changing circumstances, to sustain us.

Therefore, I am grateful that substantial healing has already taken place and will continue as we have all made a decision that we will not succumb to despair but will embrace life with optimism and hope. Deciding to heal is a necessary component when emotional healing is at stake.

However, both Neil and Jaclyn expressed how difficult it was, even weeks and months after Shawn's death, to laugh or feel good without feeling guilty. It was as if, after such a tragic and hurtful event, it was not proper to ever laugh again. Expressing this to each other, and realizing that Shawn would never wish us not to feel pleasure in our lives because of him, was instrumental to substantial healing. However, it took some time before even brief times of delight were able to overcome the prevailing sadness that was, and still is, our companion.

The Impact of Memories

I am also aware that one of the recommended coping methods for recovering from such a loss is the conscious remembering of pleasant memories. I am grateful for the wonderful memories we all have of Shawn. However, remembering even wonderful memories is a two-edged sword. On the one hand, it revives pleasant feelings of that person when they were alive and can ignite some of the images of joy and pleasure within us that the person brought into our lives. Jaclyn shared that it is the little things she remembers fondly, like a quiet drive in the car with Shawn, which can bring a smile to her face. It is true that memories are one gift of God that death cannot destroy. But memories, especially pleasant ones, also increase the awareness of the person's absence and can trigger an intense sense of loss and separation and the accompanying feelings of acute sadness. I treasure the tremendous memories I have of Shawn, but they also increase my missing him and may intensify the pain I feel at his absence. I am realizing more every day how complex and disjointed this whole grieving process is. The feelings ebb and flow, increase and decrease—every day brings something new. We feel so sad and despairing one moment and can be laughing the next. Even during the laughter, I am still aware that my son is gone and deep down my heart breaks again. That I cannot change.

Memories seem most acute when associated with specific events or dates. The first year after the loss is the year of "firsts." On his first birthday after his death, April 9, 1999, we noted he would have been twenty-eight on that day. It was so hard to realize he "would have," not "he is." Christmas 1999 was the first one without Shawn. We felt his absence keenly as we attended the Christmas Eve service at our church and later gathered together in our family room to sip hot apple cider and open one gift as is our tradition. Sharing with each other happy memories of Shawn was comforting but still difficult to handle as his absence was reinforced in our minds. Perhaps the most difficult "first" was the first anniversary of the death being such a terrible reminder of what had happened.

I remember the first time we went to the grave site. As Shawn had died in January, it was not possible to actually bury him until later in the spring. We received a call from the funeral home in the spring that the actual committal would take place, and so Peg,

Neil and I went to the cemetery to witness the internment (Jaclyn was still in Orlando). We prayed and then lowered the casket into the grave. The terrible anguish we had experienced at his death immediately returned as we witnessed his body actually being lowered into the ground. We held each other and wept over our departed son and brother, experiencing so acutely once again the pain of separation. It was a comfort, even in our grief, to know as we watched the coffin being lowered that Shawn was with his heavenly Father and also, that same heavenly Father was with us, giving the strength needed.

Since I believe that Shawn is gone and what remained was just the shell he occupied, going to the grave is not that meaningful to me. However, we have gone occasionally to the grave, either alone or with one other family member. It has not been our practice to go regularly as a family. I am much more conscious of Shawn in other significant places; the cemetery has no association with him. It only contains his shell.

However, we did go to the grave as a family after the lettering was put on the headstone. I guess each individual and family must handle these things in ways that are most comforting for them. For me, gathering as a family and sharing with each other in our home, surrounded by warm reminders of Shawn, is much more meaningful than gathering at a piece of ground in a cemetery. I know this is not the case with others who have also suffered loss and with whom I have shared. Gathering at the grave is very comforting as they seem to sense the presence of the loved one more warmly there.

All in all, tremendous healing has taken place in our lives over the last three-and-a-half years. We thank the Lord we are much better now than we were earlier. Life is certainly worth living and still has many joys which we experience individually and share together. Although we still experience moments of pain and sadness because of Shawn's death which may always be a part of our existence, we accept that as part of life in a fallen world and are still determined to live life to its fullest.

The Anguish of Lost Potential

As we have sought to promote healing and emotional growth in our lives, the terrible reality of lost potential resulting from Shawn's death haunts us still. Perhaps the greatest struggle that is initiated when a young person dies is the elimination of future possibilities and consequently, the tremendous pain caused by what will never be. It certainly is a factor as we consider long-term healing. Often, when viewing something I know Shawn would have enjoyed, when taking part in an activity Shawn would have relished, when realizing that a certain position would have been so suited to him, my heart just breaks at the realization it can never happen. Any future interaction with my eldest son is no longer a possibility in this life. We will never share any of those activities we loved, we will never discuss issues in which we both held an interest, I will never hug him in this life, we will never laugh, cry, dream or plan together as long as I live. We will have no grandchildren from our eldest son who would have made such a wonderful, loving husband and father. I will never drop by his house to see him and his family. He will never sit with us around our Thanksgiving table. There will be no more Christmases with his presence. I am continually haunted and deeply saddened by all those things that will never be. Each day, I grieve for those things I will never be able to say. As I look back, there are so many words I wish I could say to him, and it hurts to contemplate the terrible silence that comes from the words I never said. As I grieve the things I did not say, I wonder if it may have made a difference. I guess we assume they know how we feel, and I'm sure Shawn did. There is still something tragic about loving, encouraging words that never get spoken and loving deeds that never get done. How unfortunate that we seldom give the flowers while the person can still enjoy them.

The hope that sustains us through all these regrets is that we will be reunited with him in heaven where he now resides with his heavenly Father. But the lost potential of such a promising life is still a terrible tragedy and makes the healing process quite different than is the case when death occurs in a different context, for example the passing of an elderly person after a full and productive life.

Chapter 4

The Healing Process

THE LAST three years have been a painful but profound learning experience for us. We have survived the initial horror of the sudden loss of Shawn and are now experiencing a healing process that is enabling us to face each day with hope and purpose. Above all, we have learned that healing needs help. It is a process that takes substantial time and effort and a deliberate decision on our part to facilitate it happening.

I know some literature advocates stages through which a grieving one needs to go. While there are emotions we all may experience when suffering the loss of a loved one—shock, denial, anger, anguish, sorrow, depression and so on—how it happens may be as individual as each person. Sometimes the impression is given that we need to go through all the stages in order. It just doesn't work that way.

A healthy recovery process begins with a decision on our part that promotes healing rather than despair. "Recovery from loss is achieved by a series of small and correct choices made by the griever" (James and Friedman, 1998:8). Our first priority is to make the choice for healing.

Secondly, we must be open to our grief and be willing to experience the emotions that grip us. Sharing our grief in a safe and therapeutic setting allows us to experience some release from the intensity of the feelings that can overwhelm our lives and can also help provide the strength to carry on. For this, we need the help of others—wonderful people who will listen and support us with their presence and prayers, and also the comfort and sustaining presence of our heavenly Father. Thirdly, we can also help others while we ourselves are recovering from our pain, for reaching out to others in their pain can assist us coping with personal pain. However, we must be careful that in our loving help to others, we do not neglect our own healing. It may be very tempting to suppress our own pain in our service to others. Fourthly, recovery is a process that is unsteady, difficult and perhaps very long. Our lives may have been impacted in ways that mean we will never be the same.

The Nature of the Process

The process of healing is anything but smooth, and we can experience various emotions at various times. We may feel shock and denial that evolve into acceptance and resolution. The next day, we may be right back to denial and shock. Emotions jumping all over the place more accurately defines the recovery process than neat, sequential stages. It is like being on a roller-coaster ride. In addition, sometimes it seems like you move one step forward and two steps back. Thank goodness it eventually becomes two steps forward for every one back, and we finally see encouraging progress on our journey to wholeness. The final stage of peaceful acceptance only emerges after much struggle, many setbacks and emotions that have switched back and forth; it happens when the heart and head can finally experience some kind of union. I'm still not sure just when that comes as my heart and head are still somewhat at odds. I don't know if I will ever be able to cognitively contemplate Shawn's death without some feelings of denial, shock and anguish. Over time, however, we do learn to cope more adequately, and perhaps that is what successful grieving is all about. It is not to deny or stifle any lingering pain, but with courage and fortitude, face the pain, experience it and emerge stronger for the effort. Courage does not involve avoiding hardship but facing it and rising above it. I guess that is why it is called "grief work." It involves tremendous effort for healing to take place.

The important thing is to give ourselves permission to grieve. We need to grieve the tremendous loss we have experienced. It is appropriate to hurt deeply, to sob uncontrollably at times, to feel the anguish of separation, to wonder if we will ever rise again from the despair in which we are submerged. We will, if we determine we are going to heal. To stay fixated in despair is toxic and blocks recovery. We must begin the recovery journey, and I am convinced the key to comprehensive healing and a return to wholeness is in the resources available to us and how we appropriate them. God's method for the healing of His children is usually not through some supernatural zapping that wipes away our troubles, pain and grief. Rather, He works through the resources He provides for us, principally, His people. We are so grateful for His resources which have facilitated our healing is such a marvelous manner.

Resources Which Facilitate Healing

Having experienced such a loss as Shawn, I have become aware of variables in the grief process that have sensitized me like no academic knowledge could. It is one thing to know intellectually about a process, about what issues must be handled, about certain factors which are important to the process, but it is quite another thing to experience it for yourself. That in no way diminishes the importance of research, of academic inquiry and study. My whole life has been dedicated to such pursuits. However, I realized how differently even my teaching became after experiencing some of the events I had previously only discussed from literature.

Working through the grieving process, which I am discovering is a continuing and very uneven process, has taught me much. Both the literature on grief and my own experience have illustrated some factors that I have found helpful in both understanding and coping with crisis, including much about how God works in such circumstances.

Many years ago, Reuben Hill (Hill, 1958) developed a model for evaluating family crises called the **ABC-X** model where **A** is the stressor event that precipitates the crisis, **B** represents the resources available to the individuals and family for handling the crisis, **C** is the meaning attached to the crisis, often a function of the resources available, and **X** is the final result or how the crisis is experienced and the reaction to it. The model has been expanded to what is called the **Double ABC-X** model where not only is the initial crisis evaluated but also what happens after the initial crisis (see diagram in Appendix 1). "Pile-up" effects, those things that can either aid or hinder long-term recovery, are also examined after the initial crisis to help predict what will be the eventual outcome. For example, suppose a family member is in a serious car accident and is hospitalized for some time. If family members are supportive of one another, if they possess adequate financial resources, have a network of friends to assist them and have a strong faith that provides spiritual comfort, they will probably survive the initial crisis fairly well and the outlook for long-term recovery is good. Because of the various factors, the crisis will be seen as an unfortunate incident from which they must work together to recover. It may actually bring the family closer together as they comfort and uplift each other. On the other hand, if the family is fractured, finances are lacking, they are somewhat isolated from any positive social network and faith is non-existent, this family will struggle through the initial crisis, and the end result could very well be the disintegration of that family unit. The crisis will be viewed as a terrible disaster, the resources are not available to cope with it successfully either in the short or long run, and the end result of the accident may be a broken home.

Therefore, the resources that families have to cope with crises are the key to this model, and I have found the resources available to myself and my family crucial to our healing from this tragedy. For that reason, I felt it might prove a very worthwhile exercise to examine what resources families can utilize to adequately work through a shattering event in that family's life.

I was watching a video on coping with death in a family when a statistic was stated that shocked me. The narrator noted that higher than 80 percent of families that experience the death of a child will not recover from it intact. This particular tragedy will facilitate the break-up of most homes in which it occurs. They will not successfully recover as a family unit from the stress, pain, trauma and heartache initiated by such a terrible occurrence. If I had been an impartial observer viewing that video, I would have seriously challenged that particular statement as I would not have believed it could be that high. In fact, I still accept such a statement with much reservation as issues like divorce are usually very complex and have multi-variable causes. However, having endured over three years of working through the grief process, and knowing somewhat of the tremendous resources—material, emotional and spiritual—that are needed to just cope with each passing day, I do know what a terrible toll such a traumatic event can take on families. I wonder if we would have survived had it not been for our faith, our closeness as a family, wonderful extended family and friends and financial help lovingly extended. Without those resources, a horrific event could have started a downward slide to further disaster.

However, since adequate coping resources can enable a family to handle even severe crisis, I do seriously challenge the notion that the death of a child will eventually lead to parental divorce. There is also evidence that a crisis can strengthen a family as they draw together in love and support for each other (Rando, 1986:29-30; Bolton, 1986:209-211). This certainly has been the case for us as we have determined that our bonds of love and caring will not be broken. We have suffered one horrific loss. We want to avoid another at all cost.

The Role of Personal Resources

A good starting point in examining those resources that impact how we cope with family and personal crises are those individual strengths and weakness we possess, since they may be very influential in helping us facilitate our long-term healing.

Each individual is unique and consequently, each individual will grieve differently. Just as our fingerprints are unique, so are our individual personalities. Therefore, each of us will handle life somewhat differently than anyone else. Although, as a sociologist, I was aware of how individual personalities emerge as the result of the interplay of both genetic and environmental factors and that no two people are exactly alike, to observe how various members of my family, myself and Shawn's friends dealt with this tragedy was very insightful. We coped as differently as our personalities, and our healing process will be just as unique within the healing parameters which are common to us all. I realized very early that "pat" answers are useless. What may work for me may not be that helpful for someone else.

While the support of family and friends, faith in God, sharing our pain with trusted confidants and encouraging the grief work to continue are important parameters for all struggling with grief, how each person appropriates these resources and facilitates the healing process may be quite variable, and individual personalities may either help or hinder that process. For example, if we are open with people, able to share our feelings with close associates and have an optimistic, positive attitude towards life in general, we can accommodate the difficult grief work with greater ease and probably with much greater success than someone who is just the opposite. I believe this may account for many of the differences in how individuals cope with personal tragedies. It may have very little to do with their level of faith and trust in the Lord. I think that sometimes, when we see one person struggling more than another who has had similar distress, we account for the differences by judging the level of their faith rather than by allowing for differences in coping ability because of personality, environmental or personal support factors. Both persons may have a deep and sustaining faith even though one may seem to struggle more than the other.

Personalities vary tremendously as do the genetic and environmental influences that shape them, equipping some to cope with a deep emotional hurt better than others—and God does not violate our personalities. He does not alter who we are in order for us to cope more adequately. I remember some years ago seeing a poster at a youth conference with the inscription: "God does not violate the human personality." I now clearly realize what that poster was trying to communicate. God did not intervene in our lives in ways that changed our natures, even if those changes could have aided us in handling more effectively the deep pain we were experiencing.

I observed within my own family substantial variations in how we managed this terrible blow. Jaclyn, while a fairly private person, readily accepts competent, outside input as she works through events in her life. Therefore, a few weeks after Shawn's death, she returned to Orlando, Florida and her position as an exchange student with the Disney Corporation where she was on a year contract working in the Canadian pavilion at Epcot. She requested a trained counselor to help her cope with what had happened, and Disney very graciously complied. Although I was apprehensive about her being so far away from her family during the weeks and months after Shawn's death, the help of her friends and co-workers in Orlando and the providing of a counselor to aid in her recovery were an answer to prayer and God's wonderful provision for her.

Neil, on the other hand, is much less inclined to request any outside help, seeing himself as quite self-sufficient. While he did share his feelings with close friends, and he and I had some very meaningful and significant conversations, seeking outside professional help, for example, was never a consideration for him. Much of his coping was on an individual, personal level. But he gives every indication of coping rather well in his own way. This was the second severe blow to Neil as he lost his closest friend in a car accident the summer after his first year in university and was in the hospital room when they pronounced his buddy, John, dead. I was worried about how this further blow would affect him. I have been encouraged at his depth of insight into his own person concerning what he has gone through, and to be honest, my sharing with him has probably been more help to me than to him as he has been able to clearly articulate some issues that I have continued to struggle with. He has also been able to share with some of his close friends which I'm sure has helped significantly.

Peg is different again. When she is distressed, she tends to withdraw and perhaps avoid confronting the issues. Her activity level declines, and she has difficulty sharing what is happening inside her with others, including myself. She becomes less expressive, and her continuing struggle with depression intensifies. Therefore, more structured avenues for coping, some external encouragement and perhaps some medical intervention are required.

I, on the other hand, cope with pain and grief by increasing my activity level. I get busy, much the opposite of Peg. I also share with trusted colleagues and friends what is happening within me and how I am experiencing the hurt. Therefore, while we are all equally in pain, we use different strategies to help us regain some sense of wholeness which has nothing to do with the quality or nature of our faith.

I also found that things that were a comfort to me before Shawn's death could still bring a measure of comfort after. For example, music has always been a source of peace and relaxation to me. If my spirit was troubled, I would listen to music and allow it to calm and relax me. After Shawn's death, I found that listening to Christian music in the evening was helpful in quieting my troubled mind. Other things may work for other people.

What is important is that we somehow initiate the grief work that is necessary to healing and the recovery process. Grief is a necessary step in recovery. To avoid or deny the anguish that is surely there results in stunted growth and inhibits the journey to wholeness and health. Although it is a hard and painful journey, it is necessary for each to travel it in their own individual way. But travel it we must.

There is a tremendous ministry lesson here. Because we all may have various coping methods, to adequately assist others with their pain we must be very sensitive to hurting people's individual characteristics and their individual ways of handling their grief and pain. Our assistance may be as varied as they are. However, the necessity of somehow expressing our pain and allowing that expressive process to help alleviate the grip of those painful feelings is valid for all in the recovery journey. How it is done may differ. It may involve sharing one's pain with a trusted friend, colleague or counselor. It may involve writing one's feelings about what has happened in a journal or diary as did C.S. Lewis after the death of his wife. It even may be helpful to write to the loved one who has died, expressing how you feel about what has happened. The important thing is to somehow express those emotions and be released from their grip. Putting words to our grief is an essential step in dealing with the pain inside us. Writing this account has been a valuable therapeutic intervention for me in my own grieving process. It has allowed me to express much of what I have been experiencing and, consequently, feel some relief from the dreadful pain.

The Role of Friends

If anything positive can come out of such a horrible event, it is the response of people to our situation. I have come to realize as never before that God chooses to use people to accomplish much of His work, including the healing of His grieving children. The role of family members and friends has been instrumental in sustaining us through these last three years. I prayed often for God to remove the devastating pain we as a family were experiencing, but the pain did not depart. At times, I felt we had been abandoned by God, but looking back, I realize His provision was there at every stage. Most of that provision was provided through people. We were not zapped by some supernatural lightning bolt that vaporized our hurt. Instead, we were surrounded by wonderful people whom God beautifully used to minister to our broken hearts. Extended family members, personal friends, the marvelous faculty, staff and student body at ABU, the Hillside Baptist

Church family, neighbours and so many other caring people assisted in our physical needs especially immediately after the death, visited us, sent cards and notes, literally wrapped their arms around us to let us know they were concerned for us, were thinking of us and were praying for us. These were real people ministering to real people, people with names, families, problems and trials of their own to whom I am indebted for their service to us and who I want to acknowledge. Healing from such a tragedy is not an objective, clinical process where we neatly go through the proper steps in the proper sequence at the proper time. While these stages and steps may be important, the crucial element involves loving, ministering people facilitating the process. It is a personal process, and that is why this account is very personal, describing actual individuals who have touched our lives.

I meet for coffee and prayer each Friday morning with three other men who are precious Christian brothers; on Saturday, we usually go out for breakfast with our wives. It has been a close, rewarding relationship for all of us as we have shared together, visited in each other's homes, prayed together and studied the Bible together. What a blessing it was to know that, on that terrible Friday morning when Peg and I had to go to the funeral home to pick out a coffin and make the necessary arrangements, Christian friends were praying to God that we would have the strength and comfort of His presence to endure what lay ahead. I thank God for Jim and Connie Hannah, Gary and Carol MacPherson and Doug and Liz Chapman.

On that terrible Thursday evening after calling family members to tell them what had happened, I called Gordon and Carol Hisey and Mike and Joyce Kaye. They have been life-long Christian friends and have been as close as any family member. The strength and comfort I experienced just knowing they were there for us regardless of the circumstances, was emotionally life-saving.

Their response was immediate. Mike booked air passage from his home in Brantford, Ontario and was in Moncton the next day. His eulogy at the funeral touched our hearts at such a deep level. Gordie and Carol, who live several kilometers from our house, were at our home Friday, and I was so grateful for Gordie's presence when I had to go back to Shawn's apartment. Their close friendship and interaction in our lives continues to be a source of strength and support. Such wonderful responses on the part of many people were the norm.

Chet MacPhail, who, for a number of years, worked as my colleague at ABU as the Associate Dean of Campus Life and had supervised Shawn when he was a Resident Assistant, had become a close and valued friend over the years. He was the first person at our door Friday morning, even before we could go to the funeral home. He cried with us and put his arms around us, sharing in our sorrow. What a blessing his presence was at that early time.

My Christian colleagues at Atlantic Baptist University became a crucial shelter in the time of storm. Their selfless accommodation of our tragedy will never be forgotten. Initially, when the news of my cancer diagnosis was revealed, Craig Carter, the Academic Vice-President and Seth Crowell, the Registrar, immediately commenced plans to facilitate my taking a medical leave of absence in order to have an operation. It was not just the work of the University's administrators adjusting to an inconvenient situation but close, supportive Christian friends, reaching out to help in any way they could. With Shawn's death three weeks later, the response from the ABU community was overwhelming. Bill Morrison, professor of psychology who has been my trusted confidante and counselor and without whose help I'm not sure how I could have made it through this ordeal, and Steve Dempster, the first person I went to after discovering Shawn's body, arranged a prayer and anointing service for Peg and me at the University. Many of the staff and faculty, with some of their spouses, gathered on a Saturday morning in the faculty/staff lounge. Peg and I arrived not knowing what to expect. Those assembled placed us in the center and gathered around us in a circle. They placed their hands on us and individually prayed for us. Bill then anointed us on the forehead with oil. It was one of the most meaningful events we have ever experienced. The love and care expressed for us that day has made a life-long impression on our hearts. A few weeks later, they repeated this marvelous act of Christian service and love. The emotional and spiritual healing we experienced was marvelous. God ministered wonderfully to our lives through His servants. Being surrounded by such a display of concern for our well-being is something we will treasure always.

It has also been a valuable lesson to me on how to more effectively reach out to hurting people. Visibly surrounding hurting people, laying hands on them and praying for them has an immediate impact. While it is very important to pray for others in their absence, it is something else to experience the touch and voices of caring people interceding with the Father on your behalf. The context where personal contact was instrumental had a powerful healing effect on us.

As a family sociologist and professor at ABU, I was concerned about my credibility within the University. Here I was involved in helping families and my own suffers the suicide of my son. What does that say about me and how my own family has functioned? I agonized over such thoughts, but the positive, encouraging and loving input from the ABU community allayed all my fears. My worst critic continues to be myself as I cannot help but second-guess what happened and how I could have prevented it. For some reason, we are usually harder on ourselves than other people are on us. I am thankful for the loving arms of God and His people that continue to hold us tight. Their support is still conveyed to us in many ways—an e-mail of encouragement, a word of kindness, an invitation to coffee, an inquiry as to how we are doing. These all touch us deeply. I now value the little things much more than ever before, for example, a card on the anniversary of Shawn's death such as we received from Seth and Dawn Crowell who have been more like family to us than just colleagues at ABU.

At our annul summer faculty/staff meetings 2001, we were discussing the importance of encouragement within our school and how we could encourage each other as a community. I was pondering this at home after our first day of meetings and was overwhelmed by the many ways I had been encouraged by colleagues. I have never been a poet nor have I been given to spontaneous verbal inspiration, but the following just flowed from my heart, each example the result of specific acts of kindness by particular people at ABU since Shawn's death.

When you held me and wept with me,
you made me feel safe.
When you listened to my pain and hurt,
you made me feel it was okay to be vulnerable and even weak.
When you shared with me your life, your hurts, frustrations,
dreams,
you made me feel trusted.
When you asked for my help,
you made me feel competent and needed.
When you, in love and gentleness, corrected and admonished me,
you facilitated change in my life and made me a better person.
When you smiled at me, talked and laughed with me, included me in activities and treated me as a friend,
you made me feel valued.
When you gathered around me, laid your hands on me and
prayed for me.
you saved my life, because, in the worst and darkest of my
days, you made me believe life was still worth living.

I could go on and on. Jim Beverley of Tyndale Seminary, an encouraging friend for years going back to when we were colleagues at Atlantic Baptist University, called from Ontario many times over the weeks following Shawn's death, encouraging, clarifying, listening and just being there in our hour of need. Wonderful friends like Ken and Miriam MacLeod (friends and colleagues for many years) and Reg and Pat Porter (Reg, my golfing buddy and Pat, Peg's crafting friend) have continued to be there for us with visits, phone calls, invitations and other loving reminders of their continuing concern. Jim and Connie Hannah, realizing it would be difficult for Peg and I to go out to a public place for breakfast on Saturday mornings (as was our custom), immediately after Shawn's death, invited us to their home instead. As we sat around their kitchen table for the next few Saturday mornings, sharing both food and conversation, we experienced love and care in a practical way that enabled us to better continue on in those dark days.

I hesitate to recount these wonderful acts of kindness as I know I may very well miss naming someone; for that I apologize. As this is a very personal account, I want to talk about those who have touched our lives, even at the risk of omitting someone who I hope will forgive me in that event.

It has been amazing over the years to notice the staying power of Christian friendships and how God will supply the right people at the right time. While studying for my doctorate in family studies at Florida State University (1979-1981), far from home and knowing no one, the Lord provided three Christian families whose company, support and love sustained us through those two years. As we interacted as families, studied together, shared our joys and hurts and provided a shoulder when needed, a bond developed that has never severed. That bond has remained over all these years as we have interacted with each other, especially through e-mail and letters. The friendships of Larry and Sandy Barlow and Bob and

Margie Schuchts in Tallahassee, Florida, and Dennis and Emily Lowe now in Malibu, California, have been very precious.

After Shawn graduated from Atlantic Baptist University, he and some friends, as a celebration of their graduation, traveled to Florida for a couple of weeks and Larry and Sandy graciously opened their home to them for part of their trip. I know it was a highlight for Shawn as he shared with us on his return home how wonderful Larry and Sandy had been to them. It was like renewing old friendships as Shawn and the Barlow children had played together years before while we parents were in university. Peg and I have visited Larry and Sandy a couple of times since Shawn's death, and their loving hospitality and comfort have been such a source of encouragement to us. I recall so vividly on our first visit after Shawn's death, the four of us sitting on their porch one beautiful Florida evening, talking and sharing together, when Larry pointed to a plaque on the side of the house overlooking the place where we were sitting. It said, "*LOVE-LAUGHTER-FRIENDS: GATHER HERE.*" He told us the plaque was a gift from Shawn during his visit a few years before. A lump came into my throat as big as a grapefruit, and tears filled our eyes as we sat there in silence, wondering why this wonderful, generous young man was no longer with us.

The uplifting letters and e-mails we have received from Larry and Sandy and Dennis and Emily have encouraged our hearts through the trying times. I guess God was providing support networks for us back in the early 1980s knowing they would be sorely needed in 1999. In April 2001, I found myself again in Tallahassee sitting at the Barlow's kitchen table, editing part of this manuscript, and I continue to thank God for their friendship. I am so grateful for how they have graciously opened their home to us and made us feel we belong.

Both Neil and Jaclyn have also expressed the crucial role of friends in coping with Shawn's death. For example, Jaclyn's best friend, Angela, drove ten hours from the university she was attending to be with her, even though she had two exams coming up in a few days. Jaclyn says she doesn't know how she would have made it without the love of such friends as Angela as well as Ross, another close friend.

I will always be grateful for Shawn's closest friends, Paul and Mike Scharnberg and Jeff Blizzard, coming to me and telling me they would take care of moving all of Shawn's things from his apartment and cleaning everything out so I would not have to handle that very difficult task. They, along with Neil, took care of that entire job. I know it must have been so hard for them as they gathered up all the reminders of Shawn they were so familiar with. I am thankful they saved me from such a painful undertaking which I doubt I could have handled at that time.

Although I have always valued friendship, considering close friends precious gifts from God with these relationships warranting much cultivation and reinforcement, my appreciation of these people in my life has increased exponentially since Shawn's death. Wonderful friends are truly priceless treasures.

The Role of the Local Church

For many, the local church has not been a supportive environment when serious trials befall, perhaps for a number of reasons. The expectations we may have of what a fairly large group can do may be unrealistic. To expect the church as a whole to meet the very personal needs of support and comfort is courting disappointment, and yet we continue to have such expectations. Many local church members know each other only on a superficial level, seeing each other at services but having very little interaction apart from that. Therefore, many members may have difficulty knowing what to say or do when other members suffer tragedies. Except for those few individuals within the fellowship with whom we have closer relationships, expressions of sympathy are probably the extent of what we can expect.

Unfortunately for some, the church experience has been very negative. Lewis Tagliaferre, in his book *Recovery From Loss*, states:

> In my period of deepest distress after losing Rosalene (his wife), I searched for support and comfort among my church family and found none to be of help. The additional shock of this turn in events led me to search beyond Western religion and I began a study of other worldwide spiritual beliefs (Tagliaferre and Harbaugh, 1990:25).

How tragic that his local church's response to his sorrow led him in other directions away from the fellowship.

I am very thankful that our experience has not been of that type. With the shock of Shawn's death still impacting us, I asked the pastoral staff of our church to handle the funeral service, leaving virtually every detail to them. My trust was well founded. The service was a marvelous testimony to all who were there, and our pastor, Jerry Reddy's message was so appropriate and meaningful. The associate pastor, Darrell Bustin, and the music minister, Holly Howe, provided just the right music. The number of the church family who came to the visiting hours and the funeral, expressing their concern and sympathy, was overwhelming. They continued over time to express their support, letting us know they were praying for us and showing their care by making a point to speak to us each Sunday at church.

Obviously, it was the smaller group of closer friends within the church who provided the more in-depth support for us; our Friday morning prayer and Saturday morning breakfast group, and Peg's Thursday morning L.I.F.T. group (a women's group that meets each week for support, fellowship and prayer). However, the overall reaction of the church was wonderfully positive. We never had a hint of "what was wrong in that family when a family specialist has a son who commits suicide." I am very thankful for the lack of judgmental expressions and have felt no hint of rejection. We continue to be an involved part of the fellowship with our credibility still intact. Our local church continues to be a place of acceptance and support for us where we feel a sense of belonging and involvement.

Indeed, it was at a monthly men's breakfast at Hillside Baptist Church about ten months after Shawn's death that I was asked to share with the men something of what I had experienced because of that terrible tragedy, and the healing process that was underway. That presentation led to an article in the September/October 2000 edition of *Faith Today*, which in turn has led to writing this book.

For most of 1999, there was a self-imposed withdrawal from any formal involvement in the local church and most other places, with the exception of ABU, as I struggled to get my bearings. Since then, I have taught Sunday School classes, have spoken several times at our evening Sunday service, have spoken in some other churches and am again beginning to plan some family workshops which has been my practice. The family of God has not excluded me at all but has extended invitations to share and participate. If I can share from my experience, one wounded heart may be used to help another.

The Role of Family

The love and support needed from immediate family members cannot be over emphasized. As Peg, Neil, Jaclyn and myself shared our pain and love with each other, it provided more comfort than I can express. We desperately needed each other, and I thank God every day that we were there for each other. The bonds of love, caring, support, sensitivity and encouragement were tremendously strengthened and remain so much stronger to this day. Our common pain brought us together in ways we had not experienced before. The hugs, the tears, the words of encouragement, the empathy, were now expressed as never before. Shawn's death impressed on us just how much we valued and needed each other. Our supportive relationships continue to be such an important element in our ongoing healing.

In addition, the loving support of our extended families was a crucial element in our survival and the subsequent healing process. The presence of caring and helpful family members was instrumental in sustaining us through many of those dark early days, and they continue to provide much caring support. As Shawn was close to many members of his extended family, they often had to suspend their own grief and anguish in order to meet our needs. Both practical and emotional help was freely extended, and I will be forever grateful for God's gift of family. There is nothing that can take its place, especially in times of crisis. For example, Peg's sister, Marion, stayed at our house for a couple of weeks after the funeral, and her assistance and presence during such a trying time of transition were invaluable. Brothers and sisters and their spouses on both sides of our families provided whatever was needed, whether practical things like food or the emotional support of their presence.

I am especially grateful to Peg's mother and father whose strong yet gentle presence was an inspiration I will always cherish. These loving grandparents, Vaughan and Jessie, whose pain at the loss of their grandchild was evident, were a constant source of strength for us as they had suffered the loss of children in their own lives and knew what we were experiencing. Having lost three children in the space of four years, they knew the terrible anguish. Jessie, not well herself, exerted herself for us with never a word of complaint. But it took a terrible toll on her. Two weeks after

Shawn's death, she was admitted to the hospital and passed away there two months later. I'm sure her selfless effort for us contributed to her own passing, but with her wonderful, giving nature, she would not have wanted it any other way. Vaughan's words of encouragement to me, coming from one who has been there, and his practical help touched me with comfort and strength at my deepest level and sustained me more than I can ever express. I thank God every day for their wonderful impact on my life.

My own dad died a number of years before Shawn's death and my mom, in her mid-nineties, died in October, 2001. She was Shawn's second mother for the first few years after his birth, looking after him during the day as Peg and I were both working full-time, and her love for him was the same as for her own children. As we were not sure she would understand what had happened at this point in her life, we never tried to explain Shawn's passing as she would know something terrible had happened without knowing exactly what it was. Also, I know if she could understand what had happened, the shock would have been too much for her. Part of me is grateful she did not have to endure such a painful experience. She was a wonderful Christian woman and is now in heaven with her Lord and Shawn.

The role of a loving family in both the survival and recovery stages of working through such an awful experience cannot be overstated. We are fortunate to have such an incredible resource. This is not the case with many family systems that are often more divisive than unifying. The value of the numerous ways our families, in effect, have put their loving arms around us and kept us from falling into despair cannot be measured. My sister, Merla, and her husband, Roy, have opened their beautiful lakeside home in Yarmouth, Nova Scotia to us as a refuge, and we have loved our times there the last couple of summers. It has been a priceless sanctuary of love and beauty for Peg and I when we needed it most.

Sharla, another sister living in Brandon, Manitoba with her husband, Gordon, has called and prayed for us. My brother, Glenn, and his wife, Pat, have been wonderful supports in numerous ways, ministering to us in their home, calling us regularly and providing extra care for our elderly mother when Peg and I were unable to. Shawn was close to their children, Andrew, Jill and particularly Scot with whom he shared a love of video games. I know Shawn's death hit them especially hard. My brother, Darrell, and his wife, Donna, who also lost a son, know what we have endured with Shawn's death.

Peg's family has been equally comforting and helpful. I have already mentioned her father, mother and sister Marian's wonderful assistance. Her brothers who live in the Moncton area, Alden and John with their wives, Margaret and Pat, have been there for us in so many practical ways. Her brother, Joe, flew all the way from Edmonton, Alberta to be with us when Shawn died. Her other two brothers, Bob with his wife Pat in Ontario, and Jim with his wife Krys in Tennessee, have called and let us know we are in their thoughts and prayers. It has challenged me to be to others what they have been to us.

The Role of Professional/Structured Help

A resource I believe we Christians may hesitate to appropriate is that of professional counseling, grief classes and other more structured ways of learning to cope. Some Christians believe that to go to such sources for help implies lack of faith in God's provision. But some of these sources may be God's provision for us, and we would be wise to utilize every valid and competent resource at our disposal. I will be eternally grateful for the competence and training of Bill Morrison that enabled him to share with me, not only as a friend, but also as a skilled therapist. Jim Beverley and

Mike Kaye, as well, are not only valued friends but are experienced counselors. Their insightful input into our lives as a hurting family has been much appreciated.

In our family, Jaclyn had access to competent counseling through her work at Disney, and I had access to several gifted and experienced people in the helping profession. Peg, on the other hand, did not have such help readily available and, with her introverted tendencies, probably needed it the most. Therefore, Peg and I enrolled in one of the grief recovery classes conducted in our city. It proved to be a very positive experience as we could share in a safe and understanding environment what we were going through. It especially enabled Peg to articulate some of the difficult feelings she was having after the death of both her son and mother. She allowed some of these emotions to surface verbally for the first time because she knew these people had gone through much of what she had and would understand. It proved to be a valuable eight weeks because, as has been stated, realizing and expressing feelings is a necessary step in the healing and coping process. There was no magic or instant solution in the group sessions, but the time proved helpful in continuing the grief work required. Sharing our particular situation with other people who had experienced similar tragedy, and feeling their empathy and concern, was very therapeutic for us. It also sensitized us to the hurt of others as we were able to empathize with the rest of the group.

Even though I have been a family therapist and have worked with hurting families, I knew I would be a very poor therapist for Peg as I was part of the hurting system and could not stand reasonably separate in aiding her cope with her feelings. A therapist must be both concerned and somewhat objective to adequately assist someone therapeutically. It is like helping someone who has fallen in quicksand. You can jump in the quicksand with the person and try to be of some comfort as you both sink beneath the surface. Or you can be very concerned for that person's welfare but stand reasonably separate and throw them a line and pull them to safety. Peg and I were both in the quicksand, and my effective help was very limited since I was attempting to cope with my own pain at the loss of my son. We were there for each other and drew closer together because of this common tragedy, but with both of us in such pain, we were limited in what we could do to relieve each other's anguish. Our own grief was so difficult to handle in those first days and weeks, we did not have the personal resources to effectively help alleviate each other's pain. It is virtually impossible to objectively cope with a situation in which you are in the middle. External help will be necessary.

We also watched some videos compiled by Christian counselors, read books and pamphlets and surfed the Internet for material—anything that would help us better understand what had happened and what was happening. It all contributed to our healing process. Over time, we began to see some light at the end of the tunnel. However, we did note that time itself does very little. It is not time that heals but how you use the time. You could be like Miss Havisham in *Great Expectations* and, because of a tragedy, sit for the rest of your life in despair and misery, and the passage of time just exacerbates the predicament. Or you can use the time productively to learn, grow, share, grieve, pray and minister which will facilitate your own healing and give purpose and hope to life. As I noted earlier, making a decision to recover is a crucial step to healing. To restate, I believe we must decide to live productively in hope, or we eventually die in despair.

The Role of Faith

Faith in God as a coping resource in times of crisis can make all the difference. By faith, we are sure of what we hope for and certain of what we do not see, secure in the knowledge that the world was formed by God (Hebrews 11:1,3) and He is still on the throne. He will never leave us or forsake us, promising His constant presence even in the most trying times (Hebrews 13:5).

The things in which we trust and have faith set the foundation for the rest of our existence. Our faith affects our perceptions, our reactions and our expectations. If the highest object of faith is ourselves, we have very little to rely on when life goes awry. But if we have a vital faith in the living God, if we have committed our lives to Jesus Christ and live under His saving grace, what a difference it makes to everything else in our lives! It becomes the reference point by which we evaluate all else. It helps us make sense of our world, it provides strength and comfort when trouble comes and it provides abiding joy and peace through it all as we rest secure in His presence that goes beyond circumstances. James Boice says that:

> Happiness is circumstantial. But not joy. Joy is an inner quality of delight in God, or gladness, and is meant to spring up within the Christian in a way totally unrelated to the adversities or circumstantial blessings of this life (Boice, 1971:187).

As I stated earlier, peace and joy from God defy life situations. Thus, the apostle Paul could have joy while in prison, and we are not devoid of joy, even with the death of a child.

My faith in God has impacted my life in very significant ways since Shawn's death. Although I went through a difficult time of questioning and confusion, I was drawn back to the Lord for strength and comfort, and that has been such an important part of my healing process. Three areas that have developed whole new meanings for me have been God's pronouncements (His Word), God's people and God's presence.

God's Pronouncements

God's Word has spoken to me in new and meaningful ways as I have wrestled with what has happened in our family. Rather than moving away from God's Word, I have been drawn more to it than ever before. I have found tremendous encouragement and comfort in God's promises and the assurance that, although we have not been immunized from disaster, God's comforting Word is there to help us through. Each morning, as I have read passages from God's Word, they had a new impact on me because of what I had gone through. The Psalms especially have been a source of comfort and assurance as I read the numerous passages about God's provision, His comfort, His love, His faithfulness, His everlasting presence. He is our shepherd (Psalm 23), our light and salvation (Psalm 27), our strength and Rock (Psalm 18), our refuge (Psalm 7, 11, 16, 46, 61, 71), our delight (Psalm 37), our protector (Psalm 41), our help (Psalm 63, 121), our comfort (Psalm 71), our strong deliverer (Psalm 140). My troubled heart has been calmed so often as I have received help from God's Word.

I am aware that we interpret things from our own perspective and in the light of our own experiences, which can have both positive and negative consequences. There is always the possibility that my experiences may influence me to interpret Scripture in ways inaccurate to the true meaning of the text. Understanding the original context of Scripture, and always interpreting Scripture by Scripture, are very important elements to better understanding what God's Word is really saying. I'm afraid we violate this often as we put our own twist on the passage. Over the years, many passages have been interpreted by personal and cultural criteria rather than biblical criteria.

On the other hand, our own experiences may also bring to life Bible passages that may have had only peripheral significance to us.

Since Shawn's death, scriptures on the nature of God, the reality of death, our hope in Christ, the comfort of His presence, the sufficiency of His grace, the sinfulness of this world, the preciousness of His promises, while very important throughout my life, have taken on a whole new character and impact. I appropriate those promises as I never did before. I claim His presence as I never did before. I cringe at the evil and darkness of this world as I never did before. I also value the hope we have in Christ as I never did before. I thank the Lord for His precious Word as I never did before.

His People

I have already dealt in some detail with the wonderful impact caring people have had on our lives as we have struggled to cope with such a terrible event. I have been sensitized as never before to God's methodology in terms of practical, emotional and spiritual help in our lives. I, like many others I'm sure, partially bought into the idea of a God who, in times of trouble, zapped us with His comfort and strength in response to our cries, and the inner turmoil somehow disappeared. If it did not, the credibility and sincerity of our faith was in question. Unfortunately in our thinking, the "peace of God, which transcends all understanding" (Philippians 4:7) was not an inner joy which prevailed even in the hard times, but a "good feeling" placed there by God. When the "good feelings" diminished or disappeared, something was wrong with our faith, and we were left with disillusionment and discouragement. In some cases, we may even reject our faith as useless and irrelevant. I believe this is a misconception on our part of how, in most cases, God operates. I have become much more aware of what the New Testament reveals about fellowship (1 John 1:7), building up one another (Ephesians 44:12,29), the edifying work of the body of

Christ (Romans 14:9), bearing one another's burdens (Galatians 6:2), portraying Christ and His presence to each other and weeping with those who weep and rejoicing with those who rejoice (Romans 12:15). I believe God meets most of our needs not through direct intervention in our lives but through other people. That in no way limits God, who can intervene in any way He sees fit. However, the evidence of our lives and the testimony of the New Testament would support the notion that God provides His healing touch in our lives primarily through His people. The Scriptures teach that we are ambassadors for Christ (2 Corinthians 5:20). If God worked mainly through direct intervention, there would be no need for ambassadors.

My deepening awareness of this has been both comforting and disturbing. I have been so comforted by God's people who I can touch, see and relate to visibly. I have come to appreciate the wisdom and compassion of God who knew I needed this concrete input into my life. I have also been convicted because of the many times I have neglected to be God's ministering person to someone else who needed a loving hand, a comforting word, some practical help or spiritual encouragement.

The New Testament model places responsibility on each of us to be God's representatives to those in need. Praying for others is very important, and we have been so thankful for the prayers of God's people on our behalf. But we are also called to put hands and feet to our prayers. That can be very difficult. So many times we are not sure what to do or say when tragedy strikes someone we know. We are tempted to fall back on "praying for them" rather than directly interacting with them in more practical and personal ways. The people who have taken the extra step for us have our undying gratitude. How beautifully they have fulfilled the scriptures advocating service to one another. I have been challenged by their example to do the same.

His Presence

I have struggled with the reality of unanswered questions and solutions not supplied by God as I have cried out in despair. It has prompted a whole new perception of how God works in severe times. Questions such as, "Where was 'the friend who sticks closer than a brother' (Proverbs 8:24) for Shawn that night?" are still not answered. I do not handle mysteries in my own life easily and have been troubled by what I can't understand. Jaclyn's wonderful perspective on this, rather then engaging in a useless exercise of trying to solve the unsolvable, is that "the Lord took Shawn by the hand and walked him into the Light." And down deep in my heart I know that, although the Lord did not approve of Shawn's actions, He did not abandon him and was with him even at the very end.

As I have read the story of Job, I have been confronted with a whole new understanding of God's dealing with His people. Although, in this story we are allowed to see behind the scenes, Job is not. He cries out to God for what he perceives as injustice. And he is right. He is being tormented, not for anything he has done but because of a cosmic situation of which he has no knowledge. When God finally speaks to him, no explanation is offered. In fact, the very questioning of God is challenged. God makes it very clear that His presence, not answers, is sufficient. I have had to accept that I will never have many of the answers I crave, but God's presence will always be here to help compensate for the other. How grateful I have been for that realization which I have experienced in times of devotion, worship, fellowship and the receiving of daily strength.

Some time after Shawn's death, I was asked by a friend if I had any experiences of God's direct, visible, supernatural intervention in my life to help me cope with Shawn's death. I had to answer that I had not to my knowledge. I was not aware of any direct revelation of God to me or my family. None was warranted as our needs were being met through people and circumstances. God was caring for us without any supernatural zapping.

However, I realized from some of my reading that the desire to have some sign that the departed one is okay, or to have some final interaction with the deceased loved one, is very common with people who have suffered such a loss. Literature contains many stories of peoples' attempts to somehow have some final contact with that one they long for so much. It may be in a dream, a vision, a voice, etc. The loss of that wonderful relationship is such anguish and torture, one longs for some kind of communication with the person no longer present. I personally have not sought to have any contact with Shawn, believing he is now with his heavenly Father, but I have cried out in my sorrow for God to assure me Shawn is in His presence.

However, Peg, Neil and Jaclyn have told me they have all had vivid dreams of Shawn, especially shortly after his death, almost to the point of sensing his presence. I, as a social scientist, am personally inclined to believe dreams of the departed one are probably manifestations of our minds as we attempt to cope with our sorrow and anguish at the separation of a loved one rather than any actual contact with the one departed. I am open to correction on this point if evidence proves me wrong.

However, since the time I was asked that question, two events have happened that I will share as I am still not sure just what they mean. I do not believe either of them were necessary to enable God to supply our needs, but I have pondered many times just what they meant and what they represented. Were they just coincidences in a world where things happen by probability (under God's permissive will), or were they a means of God's compassionate benevolence to me and my family?

The first incident happened one morning a few weeks after the death. I was greatly troubled in my spirit and experiencing terrible anguish. I got out of bed and was walking down the hallway, and I cried out to God to help me. Immediately, I was flooded with a peace and comfort that was amazing. The terrible anguish of the moment was instantly gone. That had never happened before nor has it happened since. I have experienced God's strength and comfort in the midst of my anguish, but to have the anguish itself immediately vanish temporarily was a unique experience. I cannot explain it, but I thank God for it and take it as a sign of His loving care.

The second incident happened a few months after Shawn's death, and I must put it into context. While Shawn was working for the Sheriff's Department, a colleague gave him a stock tip to the effect that a penny stock was probably going to do well. Shawn passed the tip on to me as he did not have much money to invest at the time. I told him I would buy a bit of the stock which was trading for $.13 per share, and, if we made anything on it, we would split it. It only amounted to a few dollars investment and was more for fun than anything else. The stock rose to $.18 per share and then did not move. We both forgot all about it, and that was that.

It was a Friday evening, months after his death, and I was feeling particularly low. I cried out to God for some assurance that Shawn was with Him and was okay. I truly believed Shawn was with his heavenly Father, but, in my sorrow and troubled emotional state, I just desired some extra assurance at that particular time. Later, I went to bed and, to be honest, thought little more of it.

The next morning, the phone rang, and it was Shawn's former colleague from the Sheriff's Office. He said he had been thinking about Shawn and had wanted to call for some time. He also had something he wished to report to me. He asked if I was aware of a stock tip he had given Shawn while Shawn had been working with him. I told him I was and that, while Shawn did not buy any, I had purchased some and forgotten all about them. He said a very extraordinary thing had happened on Friday, the day before. For some reason he did not know, the stock jumped from about $.18 per share to $.70 per share. He called me to let me know. I thanked him, and we ended our conversation. Again, I did not think much about it.

It was Monday, back in my office, when I decided to check out what I had been told. I called the broker, and he confirmed that the stock had taken an unexpected jump. As I hung up the phone, I was overwhelmed by the impression in my mind of "You asked for assurance, I have given it to you." I was dumbfounded. It was only then that I connected my plea on Friday with the subsequent events with the stock. Was it just coincidence that the stock jumped the day I asked for assurance? Was it coincidence that I received the phone call from Shawn's colleague the next day, saying he was prompted to call? Was my impression on Monday just wishful thinking? Of course I cannot say for certain, but I am convinced it was God again encouraging my troubled heart.

Was it necessary for God to do it? Not at all. I do not presume a sovereign God should act as I see fit. But I am very grateful for the love and care I believe He revealed in a unique way. His watchful provision for us is ever-present, regardless of how He provides it. I have received no dreams where Shawn has appeared from the other side, I have had no visions nor have I heard any voices. Personally, I believe God will supply what we need without any direct contact, in whatever form, from Shawn. If Shawn is with his heavenly Father, as I believe, I cannot expect direct communication from him. I do not argue with others who report such occurrences, but for me, such things have not taken place.

I continue to thank God for His faithfulness and am so grateful that this whole experience has not led to bitterness and loss of faith even in the face of such a difficult spiritual struggle. In fact, it has drawn me closer to the Lord as I have needed His strength and comfort. Prayer has become more meaningful and significant as a daily part of my life. God's presence has given strength to carry on in the present, comfort to handle the past and hope to face the future. Without my faith, life would have been virtually unbearable. Our faith as Christians is not a blind faith but is based upon a faithful God who has proven faithful time and time again. Faith is only as valid as the object in which it is placed, and our faith is placed in the sovereign God, creator and sustainer of the universe, who has demonstrated His love by the gift of His son, our Lord Jesus. I do not understand much of what has happened and may never in this life. I do know that God, while allowing Shawn's death by His permissive will, has not abandoned us in our grief but has sustained us each step of the way.

I have been incredibly thankful for the resources that have been available to me and my family which have made the healing process both possible and probable. There are many suffering deep anguish who may not be so blessed. Family, friends and finances may be in short supply, thus the road to recovery difficult indeed. Please be encouraged that all is not lost. First, God's strength, comfort and sustaining grace are available to all. He has promised that all who come to Him, He will never reject but will take their cares on Himself as He cares for us (Matthew 11:28; 1 Peter 5:7). Secondly, contact and reinforce any relationships that may be available to help sustain you through your grief. It may be a particular family member, an acquaintance, a neighbour, a colleague. Usually, we all have someone if we look hard enough. Thirdly, seek out any formal or organized help that may be available. This could be grief groups, social agencies, church groups, clergy, counselors, any specific resources that the community at large may offer. They can be of tremendous help, both in addressing the grief being experienced, and also in facilitating contact with other people in similar circumstances who can add personal support. Make a decision that you are going to do all you can to enhance you own recovery. God has placed amazing personal resources within the human spirit that can accomplish marvelous things when we decide to utilize them.

Chapter 5

Suicide–The Unnatural and Unexpected

THE NATURE of Shawn's death has been one of the most difficult aspects of this whole tragedy for us as a family. It has been the prime factor in my personal struggle to understand what happened. There seemed to be little or no warning, and the shock of him taking his own life reverberates still. In my effort to better understand why my son chose to do this, I was prompted to further investigate why anyone would end their life. Although I have done some work in this area because of my position as a family sociologist, my own experience with Shawn motivated me to examine the literature as I had not done before. Suicide is a very complex issue with no easy or simple answers. With some incidents, there seems to be a pattern whereby the end result can almost be predicted, while in other cases, the death seems to defy reason and all indicators. The survivors are left with a profound mystery as well as the loss of the loved one. Grief is compounded by the method of death.

Suicide is one of the leading causes of death in North American society. In the US, for example, it is the eighth leading cause of death for all Americans and the third leading cause of death among young people aged fifteen to twenty-four (Surgeon General's Report, 1999). More people die from suicide than homicides. In Canada, there are 30,000 suicide attempts each year and, on average, 4000 people succeed (Evenson, 2000). This is such a depressing statistic and so difficult to accept, especially concerning young people. Students of suicide do not seem to provide many answers for its occurrence. The more I have examined this phenomenon, the more perplexed and confused I have become. As I have read about the reasons for suicide, they seem more like the circumstances we all face each day. We all are depressed at times; we all face difficulties; we all have to handle uncertainty and hardship; we all have experienced failed relationships; and on it goes. This is not a list of causes for suicide; this is everyday life for most of us, yet we do not all commit suicide. Shawn's life differed very little from most of those around him. In fact, his life was in many ways much better than many he knew. But they are still here, and he is gone. I cannot explain that.

The literature discusses signs that we are to recognize, and in some people, they may be very evident. When people talk about how unhappy they are, how they do not want to live and so on, we had better take what they say and do very seriously. I once had a student who was involved in an accident that took the life of his fiancée. He blamed himself for her death, and eventually the guilt became unbearable, leading him to commit suicide. The signs were there and, although close friends hesitated to believe that suicide could ever be an option, even in this case it was.

For the majority of suicides, there are signs that suicide may be a possibility. Yet there are many suicides that do not conform to the norms we set for that behavior. There are times when the signs are not visible, when there seems no cry for help, when circumstances do not warrant that extreme action, when lack of friends and loved ones is not an issue, when stress and difficulties do not seem overwhelming and when faith in God is present. These are the ones that present so much difficulty in understanding. I have talked with students who have experienced tremendous difficulty ranging from severe abuse, rape and extreme financial hardship, to broken dreams and shattered relationships, but these students are still here. Taking their lives was not an option.

Why suicide was an option for Shawn—with his upbringing, his academic training, his intelligence, his experience, his friends and family, his faith, his personal resources—is a baffling mystery. To end your life when on the verge of fulfilling a project you have planned for and dreamed about seems completely contradictory. But somehow, in the mind of Shawn, it was not. That is what I cannot comprehend. The decision to take one's life is made because of inner perceptions that person has of reality that may not logically correlate to external circumstances. The world in the mind of the suicidal person is not the real world but a radical distortion of it. Yet we try to understand based on what we can observe and with which we can relate, and usually that is the external circumstances. From the outside, Shawn seemed to be doing well, but obviously, from his inner perspective, that was not the case, and we did not have access to much of that inner world which he kept hidden. We still wonder why he chose to deal with his inner turmoil by himself rather than sharing his anguish with us.

Charles Swindoll relates the story of the University of Nebraska football player, Brian Hiemer (*Growing Deep in the Christian Life*) that was printed in *Sports Illustrated*, September 1985. Brian was an all-state football player in high school and, when he was cut in his freshman year at Nebraska, he persuaded coach Tom Osborne for another chance. He rapidly rose to a first string player, having a great season. Just before his senior year commenced, he visited his home, a large farm in Shelby, Nebraska, arriving Friday evening, August 9, 1985, just before he was to return to the university for fall training camp. He walked the fields with his father and, although quiet, gave no indication that anything was seriously wrong. But on Tuesday afternoon he walked behind a wooden shed and killed himself with a .22 caliber rifle. His father stated that he looked for a reason, but Brian never indicated any to them. The article notes: "Hiemer is gone, and no one understands the reason. Huey says, 'Whatever it was, it will rest with Brian.'" Swindoll continues: "Frankly, that could be your son… or mine" (p. 373). For us, it was our son, and we are as perplexed and shocked as were the Hiemer family, the town of Shelby, Nebraska and the Cornhuskers football team of Nebraska University. It does not seem to make any sense.

So for us, the most horrific aspect of this tragedy, and the most difficult to understand, is that Shawn took his own life. In many ways, suicide is more problematic to cope with than other types of death, especially when it is the death of a young person. Even though death for any reason is hard to accept, it is a part of life and we all know that eventually it will claim each of us. However, death because of suicide or the death of the young are often unexpected and viewed as somehow "unnatural" since there was so much of life yet to be lived. My dad died at the age of ninety after a long and productive life. As difficult as it was, it was expected and seen more as a home-going than a tragedy. He was a Christian and was ready to go meet his Saviour. In fact, his death was seen as both a loss and a blessing as we did not want to see someone who had been so active all his life remain bedridden for any length of time with no hope of recovery. It was the same for my mom.

The death of a young person presents a whole different scenario. It seems so out of the norm, so contrary to what we expect.

It dashes hopes, it cancels dreams, it seems more like a tear in the fabric of time than the natural consequence of the passage of time. The reaction is very different. Our grief at Shawn's death was so different than what we experienced with my dad. We mourned the loss of my father and mother, but the depth of grief experienced from those events did not compare to what we experienced when Shawn died. The day after he died, I went back to his apartment with one of my closest friends, Gordon Hisey, to gather up some things before the apartment was cleaned. As we drove through the city, Gordie put it all in perspective when he stated through his grieving heart (as he had known Shawn since his birth), "This is not how it is supposed to be. Our children are supposed to bury us, not the other way around."

There is something even more unnatural when the death of the young person is a suicide. When sickness or accidents take the lives of our children, the pain is unbelievable. I do not believe the method of death makes any difference to the pain we experience. We have still lost a child, and that reality is not modified by the way it happened. When my brother, Darrell, and his wife, Donna, lost their two-year-old boy in a car accident, I'm sure their pain was as deep as that which Peg and I felt with Shawn's loss. Our Christian friends and neighbours, Michael and Rennie Roop, lost their two teenage boys in a horrific highway accident less than a year after Shawn's death, and their grief will be every bit as deep as anyone can experience.

Indeed, losing all one's children at one time wields a blow like nothing else on earth. Even with the horror of Shawn's death, we have two more children to help fill the gap. My heart still cries for Mike and Rennie as their loss goes beyond what I can imagine. However, we do grieve the loss and handle the pain differently when it is a suicide. I believe this is true for a number of reasons.

1. You grieve both the loss of the loved one and the method by which it happened.

With suicide, a double blow has been dealt. You not only grieve the loss of the loved one who has died, which is so painful in itself, but you also must cope with the fact that the death was deliberate. When one dies and there is nothing we can do about it, there is still tremendous grief. When sickness, old age, an accident, etc. take the lives of family members and friends, we hurt for the loss and grieve for them. We know that, in a fallen world, accidents, old age and sickness are part of the reality we must face every day, and there is almost nothing we can do about them. However, in these cases, the loved one did not make a decision to leave us. Although their loss is just as painful, we are not left with the terrible reality of why that loved one decided to take their own life. And even though suicide is not uncommon in our society, the realization that the person chose to end their life impacts those left behind as nothing else can.

2. The question "Why?" becomes more pervasive.

We have tried to make some sense of it and answer the "why" regarding Shawn's death without much success. The question becomes more haunting when the one who chose to die had so much to live for. Perhaps part of the answer lies in the particular biochemistry of the person involved. Some new research in neurobiology indicates that particular individuals may be predisposed to suicide because of biological triggers in the brain or even because of a defective gene. If this is so, when certain environmental factors are present, the natural preventive mechanisms against self-destruction may be absent or weakened in some individuals. Studies by scientists at the Royal Ottawa Hospital claim that a mutated gene may lead to suicide. The researchers found a mutation in the gene encoding for the serotonin 5-HT2A receptor, a protein that transmits brain signals. They claim that the mutation more than doubles the risk of suicide in persons who carry it (Evenson, 2000). J. John Mann of Columbia University and the New York State Psychiatric Institute has focused his studies on this neurotransmitter, serotonin, and has noted that low levels of the neurotransmitter is linked with those who make the most lethal attempts on their own lives. Mann's colleague, Victoria Arango, has found additional evidence that diminished serotonin activity is linked to suicide (Leutwyler, 1997).

We will never know if genetic and biochemical factors had an influence on Shawn's behavior, but talking to other family members and people who have attempted suicide or dealt with individuals who have, the biological element cannot be disregarded. One individual who survived a very serious attempt on his own life described the event to his father as a black wave that flowed over him, and he could think of nothing else except ending his life. All other considerations seem irrelevant. When this individual was asked if he thought of the consequences for those he would leave behind, he said those considerations never entered his mind. Knowing Shawn and his caring nature, I believe he, too, was somehow blocked from realistically considering the heartache his death would cause. It would seem that brain chemistry somehow altered his normal defenses and perceptions. Mann's research points to mixed-up chemical messengers in the prefrontal cortex, an area of the brain involved in processing emotions and inhibitions. He goes on to say, "New research indicates that suicide is not a normal response to severe distress" (Leutwyler, 1997).

Does this mean that Shawn had no choice, and that he was not responsible for what happened? Not at all. Even a predisposition does not determine that an event must happen. But it does provide another variable in understanding what happened and additional information that may help prevent similar occurrences in others in the future. We still are reasoning creatures and must take responsibility for our actions, except perhaps in cases where we are severely incapacitated. Shawn still made a terrible decision. But I believe there were biological factors that contributed to the decision by blocking some of the consequences of his action and the natural inhibitions against self-destruction.

And, although I am not inclined to see a demon behind every bush and feel that "the devil made me do it" is often used to relieve us of responsibility, I certainly do not rule out the forces of evil acting on Shawn who may have been in a weakened state due to business pressures, discouragement, etc. Our great enemy, Satan, still prowls this world wrecking havoc wherever possible, and the death of a young Christian would not displease him at all. However, I did not see any evidence that Shawn was under any kind of direct satanic influence.

I have imagined over and over what may have been going through his mind just before that fateful moment. The brief note he left told us that he loved us and he did not want us to hurt for him. He wanted to be with his Lord and Saviour. Was the prospect of heaven so much better than staying here on earth that he felt he must go? Did he say goodbye to us? Why did he not come for help? What was happening in his life to make it not worth living? The questions, most of which will never be answered, are numerous.

3. There is increased fear for other family members.

As I discussed earlier, although parents have a natural concern for our children's well-being and a healthy fear for their safety and welfare, the suicide of a child opens a fear that goes far beyond reasonable concern. I found that I not only had to deal with my

Suicide—The Unnatural and Unexpected

anguish over the death of my son, I also had to cope with the debilitating fear that my other children might do the same thing. That prospect was absolutely terrifying. Part of our long-term healing has been to open this issue as a family and greatly diminish the prospect that it could ever happen again. I pray daily that this will be the case. I am so thankful that, at this time, my grief over Shawn is no longer exacerbated by paralyzing fear for other family members.

4. With a suicide, grief is accompanied by substantial guilt.

The death of a child cannot help but generate substantial guilt in parents. It is natural, as caregivers, to ask ourselves where we went wrong regardless of how the death occurs. As I discussed previously, this is greatly increased when the death is a suicide, and I have wrestled with this terrible reality until I have virtually collapsed. It has been a difficult journey to achieve a measure of healing in this area. But it has happened, and guilt's stranglehold on my life no longer exists.

The process to substantial healing of guilt has involved a number of factors. In my mind, I have examined the relationship between Shawn and myself to ascertain if there were elements that could have contributed to his death. I am so grateful for the loving and supportive bond that existed between us. Although I don't see how the pain could have been worse, I do believe the struggle would have been much more difficult if, for some reason, Shawn and I had been alienated from each other. The subsequent guilt and remorse would have been overwhelming if I felt that a strained relationship between us contributed to his death.

Why our close bond did not motivate him to share his troubled state of mind is still a mystery to me. I believe he probably did not want to burden me further with his problems when I had just been diagnosed with cancer and, in his distorted mindset, felt his going would ease some of the pressure. Of course, it did just the opposite.

I have also pondered at length the larger context of his life to try and discover if there were severe enough variables impacting him to warrant such action on his part. I have found none except those that effect us all as we cope with both the joys and difficulties of day-to-day living. I have examined my behavior towards Shawn, others' behavior towards Shawn, anything that might help explain what happened, but I have come up blank. I have uncovered nothing that would have produced his death. Were there stresses, difficulties, problems, habits, discouragements, etc.? Of course! But, as Neil noted, there was nothing that could have remotely predicted what happened. It has been an exasperating but necessary process for me as I have second-guessed myself all along the way.

Over time, I began to realize that all my perceptions and evaluations were set in the context of what had already happened. I was examining the past by the present and feeling substantial guilt for not preventing what happened. Therefore, I mentally placed myself back in the past, before Shawn's death, to see if there were factors that I ignored, down-played, avoided, etc. where, if I had reacted differently, I could have prevented his self-destructive behavior. Given that context, I honestly felt I would probably have acted no differently than I did, as neither myself nor others close to Shawn were aware of anything that could have produced that fateful Thursday evening. Hindsight is twenty-twenty, but, when in a present situation, it is not nearly so clear. As I look back and interpret things from the past by what has subsequently transpired, I do see things I wish I looked at differently then. I would have been much more sensitive to Shawn's life, to what was happening to him, the pressures he was under and so on. However, the idea of suicide was not even remotely in my mind, so acting in that awareness did not exist. I finally realized I could not blame myself, or anyone else, for what we did not know or could not even imagine. It took a lot of difficult soul-searching to come to that point in the healing process.

Going through this exercise produced substantial relief of the inappropriate guilt that had gripped my life. Although it still took some time for my head to at least partially convince my heart that it was not my fault nor the fault of others close to Shawn, I believe this was a very beneficial exercise on my road to recovery. I am so grateful for many wonderful close friends and family members who, by their encouraging comments, helped confirm that we as a family, or others close to Shawn, were not factors in his decision to end his life. The mystery of why, however, remains intact.

Chapter 6

Death—The Great Enemy

THIS EXPERIENCE has forced me to reflect, as never before, on the reality of living in a fallen world where sickness, evil and death are the norms and eventually impact all of us, perhaps in very terrible ways. I realize that death for the Christian has different connotations than for the non-Christian because, as Christians, we have the wonderful hope that departing this life means entering the presence of our Lord. Death is also an inevitable part of life whether we like it or not. But it is the last great enemy that God will destroy (1 Corinthians 15:26), and that enemy exists because we live in a sinful and fallen world. The Bible states that the wages of sin is death (Romans 6:23), and I have been gripped by the obscenity of death and just how terrible it can be. The death of a child, chronic illness, horrific accidents and other tribulations are the results of living in a sinful world, and they inflict pain and heartache on all of us.

Life, however, is the gift of God, and therefore these hurtful situations cannot be the intentional acts of a vengeful God seeking evil against us "for our own good." Consequently, we should never ascribe good to evil, regardless of the end results. I have struggled with this as I have reflected on God and Him allowing such terrible things to happen. I have to believe that Shawn's tragic death broke the heart of God just as it did ours. "His heart is touched with *our* grief" ("Does Jesus Care," Hymn by Frank Graeff). Although God allows such events and does not often overrule our actions (even the self-destructive ones), they are part of a sovereign God's permissive will, not part of His active, intentional will. His sustaining presence, power and provision are there for us when these terrible things happen, providing the strength and comfort we need to endure such horrible experiences.

But Shawn's premature death will remain a horrendous tragedy, regardless of what positive things may come from it. The idea that evil is actually good because something positive may come from a terrible event is erroneous. We should never ascribe good to evil. It is one thing to see good emerge from an evil situation, but it is quite another to see the evil, therefore, as good. R. C. Sproul (Sproul, 1982) has observed that even the assertion, "All things work together for good" in Romans 8:28 (KJV) is a testimony to the power and triumph of God over real death-dealing evil, not a signal that evil is really good in disguise. Whether the good which emerges from many evil situations can ever overcome the harm created by those situations in this life, is doubtful. We may have to wait until glory for "all things to work together for good."

We must never credit God with the evil because good has emerged. God can bring positive outcomes from very unfortunate events, but to believe that God orchestrated the evil so that good could transpire is contrary to Scripture. Job 34:10,12 states: "Far be it from God to do evil, from the Almighty to do wrong.... It is unthinkable that God would do wrong." Our heavenly Father cannot initiate evil for any purpose. It is contrary to His very nature. The psalmist makes it clear that our heavenly Father is "not a God who takes pleasure in evil" (Psalm 5:4). Although God, by His permissive will, may allow tragedy to befall us because even we, His children, live in this fallen world, the concept of God as the originator of evil, who crushes us with misfortune to somehow teach us a lesson, has no support in the revealed truth of His Word. Even in the case of Job, God may have allowed disaster to occur, but we must remember it was not God performing the terrible acts. A loving God who sent His Son to die for us and yet somehow delights in our trials and tribulations would be a God whose nature is at odds with itself. God cannot be a contradiction within Himself. I do not understand much of the nature of God, the subtle distinctions between His permissive will and active will, how all-knowing is distinguished from determining. I do know that God did not orchestrate Shawn's death even though He allowed Shawn's terrible action to proceed without His interference. He allowed Shawn to make a disastrous decision and did not overrule him. Most of us have made unfortunate decisions that God did not overrule, and I believe this is God's normal methodology most of the time. There is none among us who would not do many things differently if we could go back in time and relive our lives.

Although God does not usually overrule our decisions, even our terrible ones, His heart was still broken by the actions of His child just as ours were. God is never pleased when we act in ways that lead to death and heartache. However, His presence, comforting and strengthening, is never absent, even in these horrific situations. I wish God had interfered with Shawn's actions and prevented that terrible evening from happening. But who am I to presume what God should do? If God violates our will to act in this case, should He also interfere in all other cases? I cannot question a sovereign God's actions, a God who can see the end from the beginning and for whom time has no limiting impact.

There have been positive things that have emerged from Shawn's death. We have been sensitized to grief and pain in others like nothing else could have done. It has brought us closer as a family as we have had to sustain one another and minister to each other. It has brought a whole new appreciation of how wonderful our friends and family can be in times of tragedy. It has allowed us to experience God's comforting presence as never before. It has compelled each of us to look closely at who and what we are as individuals. I will never forget Neil's comment a few days after Shawn's death; he said that this painful event must make us all more loving. What a comfort it was to me to see such an incredible perspective in Neil just after the death of his brother.

Have the positive aspects been worth it? I must confess I would gladly exchange all the positive things that have transpired if I could have my son back! Although I am grateful for the good we have experienced because of this painful event, and how God has allowed ministry opportunities to help make up for some of the hurtful consequences, it cannot compensate for the ache in my heart that never goes away or the absence of my son, who, in this life, I will never see again.

Death also has a wide-ranging impact like ripples spreading out across a pond caused by some movement on the surface. Shawn's death not only caused us, his immediate family, incredible pain, but the hammer blow was felt in our extended family, among Shawn's friends, family friends, his working colleagues, the local church, the Atlantic Baptist University and Acadia University communities and beyond. We received responses from all over North America. I was astounded by the impact one death had on so many people, partly, I believe, because it was a suicide. The consternation and disbelief it caused in so many people who knew him well were common reactions. Like us, virtually all who interacted with us those first few days struggled to believe such a thing could happen. It just did not seem possible. And to be honest, at times it still seems more like a bad dream than a real event that actually happened.

Having your child die causes one to reflect on what it must be like "on the other side." What kind of place is it? We have some images from Scripture, but they seem more like concepts expressed in terms we can readily understand than a comprehensive picture of an actual place. Is time no longer a relevant consideration? Will there be family reunions in heaven? There is little in Scripture to support any notion that our earthly family structures will survive the grave. What is it really like to "be like Jesus" when we see Him as He is? Is Shawn's essence—the part which left his earthly body—in a new body now? Is it a spirit, conscious in God's presence? Does he feel sorrow for what has happened? Things I never really gave much thought to or questioned before, I have pondered deeply in recent times.

I also have found nothing noble or uplifting about death. It is still the scourge of the human race and the initiator of tremendous pain and heartache. There may be nobility in how some people die, for example, giving one's life for others or in a great cause, but death itself is still the great enemy. Misfortunes, sickness and death are terrible realities in a world characterized by sin. Experiencing the death of a child, however, has given me a whole new appreciation for the life we have in Christ. And I praise God for His indescribable gift that we have in our Lord, Christ Jesus (2 Corinthians 9:15). What a despairing place it would be if the horror of death was not countered by the wonderful life we can have in Jesus. Because of the death of Christ, our own experience of death, as horrible as it is, can be the gateway to life with our Saviour.

Chapter 7

Rediscovering God

UR EXPERIENCES are filters through which we view our world. Someone who has endured extreme hardship sees the world much differently than someone who has had a smooth time of it. It is the same with spiritual perceptions. Our view of God is influenced by our personal world and the events that have characterized it. Even interpretations of Scripture are impacted by individual and cultural perspectives.

A dramatic shift in our personal world may have a tremendous impact on our perspectives, altering them significantly. Since Shawn's death, I now view many things very differently because of that traumatic, hurtful experience. It has also caused me to reexamine my view of God—who He is, how He operates, what characterizes His person.

I grew up in a church that had a fairly balanced view of God for which I am thankful. We were taught about the love of God, about His mercy and grace, about His watchful care. We were also taught about His majesty, His sovereignty, about His justice and, most importantly, about His holiness. I realized very early that my loving heavenly Father was also the holy, awesome creator of the universe who demanded respect, awe, worship and praise. Tony Campolo, speaking at an Urbana Missions Conference (Tape of address), notes that God created us in His image and we, as a society, have decided to return the favour. So we create God in our own cultural image, far removed from the God of the Bible. He is not "the man in our corner," "the guy upstairs," the benevolent grandfather satisfying our every desire or the disinterested observer, winking at our calamities, amused at our transgressions. To trivialize God in these ways contravenes the portrayal of God revealed in Scripture. I still cringe to hear people so casually say, "Oh my god."

Because of my pain and sorrow, I have gone back to the Bible in a way I had not done before. I needed comfort, assurance, emotional and spiritual strength, hope and solace as I had never needed them in my life. What I found was much more than I initially sought. I saw anew the God of Scripture, the high and lifted up One who is still mindful of us, who never leaves or forsakes. While He is the loving heavenly Father, He is also the God of creation and is not answerable to me any more than He was answerable to Job. While it has been hard, at times, not to hold God accountable for what happened, as I have struggled with placing blame and responsibility for the terrible events which have devastated our family, my learning over the past three-and-a-half years has allowed me, to a certain extent, to let go, to accept things as they are and leave many of the answers in the hands of a sovereign God.

It has not been easy. As I related earlier, I have reread J.I. Packer's book *Knowing God*, I have pondered Philip Yancey's books, relating to him when he states:

I tend to write as a means of confronting my own doubts. My book titles—Where Is God When It Hurts, Disappointment With God—betray me. I return again and again to the same questions, as if fingering an old wound that never quite heals. Does God care about the misery down here? Do we really matter to God?" (Yancey, 1995:17).

As I read Colson's book, *How Now Shall We Live,* I realized anew that we live in a world characterized by major contradictory worldviews, and it compelled me to reexamine my own stand as a Christian. Reading R.C. Sproul's *Reason to Believe* has strengthened and encouraged my heart. Watching and listening to Dr. Bill Bright's series on the characteristics of God has again expanded my understanding of God and reacquainted me with the God of Scripture.

Out of all of this has emerged a new appreciation for who God is. Some of the obvious truths about God, about which the Scriptures are very clear but which, I believe, we often neglect to consider, have become much more instilled in my consciousness.

God's Ways Are Not Our Ways

In our attempt to make God in our image, we fail to fully comprehend just how different He is. For me to understand how God works is impossible, as He operates in ways I will never be able to comprehend (Isaiah 55:8). I, as the creature, cannot discern how the creator operates. I have not had any problem with this when considering the mysteries of the universe and how God has seen fit to work in human history. I may wonder why, but I can accept God's uniqueness as the master of creation and history. It is another story when I cannot understand why my son is dead. All at once, it has become very personal, affecting my family and me in profound and painful ways. Not to understand all of how God has shaped human history may be mysterious and intriguing, but not to understand why my son, a child of God, was not prevented from such a terrible act, is exasperating. I have had to finally accept that God works in ways I cannot fathom, even in the micro areas of our lives. To ultimately leave it in the hands of an all-knowing God is difficult but essential, and it has taken some time. To cast even this care on Him for He cares for me has been both difficult and freeing.

His Perspective is Not Ours

Just as God operates in ways we cannot comprehend, so His perspective is vastly different from ours. I have had to realize once again that God stands apart from time and sees the end from the beginning. This perspective I cannot even imagine. God's perspective encompasses all of history simultaneously. Shawn's birth, life and death are all within God's immediate perspective. He is not constrained at all by time as we are. He stands apart from time. He is the alpha and omega, the beginning and the end (Revelation 21:6). To attempt to fully understand what has happened from God's perspective is an exercise in futility. Again, we leave it in the hands of a sovereign God. The role of faith becomes absolutely crucial as we contemplate what has happened and the nature of God. We may not be able to comprehend all of God's perspective, but our faith in who He is, and that He is absolutely faithful and loving, is a comfort like no other.

He May Not Overrule Our Decisions

When God created us in His image, that involved making us reasoning, responsible creatures, capable of making our own decisions. This is both wondrous and frightening. While we can decide freely to serve and love God, we can also decide to reject Him. We can make both good and bad decisions. We see this back in Genesis when Adam and Eve chose to disobey God. The human race has suffered the disastrous consequences of that decision ever since. This in no way limits God. He is free to do as He wills, which includes overruling any human decision. Experience, however, tells us that in most cases, God does not overrule our decisions, even the terrible ones. The Bible is full of stories about wrong decisions and the consequences of those decisions. God is our shield and defender (Psalm 28:7, 144:2, Proverbs 23:11), the friend who sticks closer than a brother (Proverbs 18:24), but does not apprehend from us the responsibility for our own behavior. He usually will not violate His own image in us. I wish, in Shawn's case, that He would have, but He did not. I have realized anew my own responsibility before God for my behavior, and that He will hold me accountable for what I do. He may not protect even His own children from disastrous decisions, just as He did not prevent His people, Israel, from folly but allowed the natural consequences of their disobedient actions to take their toll.

I have had difficulty correlating my view of parenthood with that exemplified by God. I try to protect my children, even from themselves, in any way I can. I will shield them from the natural consequences of wrong decisions and bail them out if necessary. It seems natural to do so. But God may not operate that way at all. Again, His ways and perspective are far above mine and exceed my understanding.

He May Not Explain His Working

In our lives, we are a lot like Job, never knowing the reasons for much of what may be happening. Although God knows all things, the present as well as the future, we do not, and we cry out in frustration and grief, much like Job. God's response to Job reveals much about what He is like. God never did explain to Job the reasons for what was happening to him. Instead, he rebuked him for questioning the creator of the universe. He spoke to him from the storm, saying, "Who is this that darkens my counsel with words without knowledge" (38:2), and continues to illustrate to Job just how limited his perspective really is. God ends by asking, "Will the one who contends with the Almighty correct him? Let him who accuses God answer him" (40:2). Job repents for his reaction to God when God makes it clear that He asks the questions, not Job.

The lesson here is not that God is uncaring and delights in the hardships of Job, but that He deserves our trust and confidence, regardless of external circumstances. No matter what is happening, God is still in control, and our doubt is the result of our lack of understanding, not God's failure. As Job realizes this, he cries out:

> "I know you can do all things; no plan of yours can be thwarted. You asked, 'Who is this that obscures my counsel without knowledge?' Surely I spoke of things I did not understand, things too wonderful for me to know. You said, 'Listen now, and I will speak; I will question you, and you shall answer me.' My ears had heard of you but now my eyes have seen you. Therefore I despise myself and repent in dust and ashes" (42:2–6).

As we struggle with so many things we cannot understand, it is difficult to leave them in the hands of a sovereign God, but we, just like Job, may have no other choice. Like Job, we may cry out for answers, but we have no claim on God that compels Him to explain. Therefore, no explanation may be the final result. We must trust God in whose hands all knowledge rests.

God Does Not Immunize His Children from Hardship

As we study Scripture, we key in on the verses that provide security and comfort which is very natural. We love those verses which state that He will never leave us or forsake us (Hebrews 13:5), that He is the friend that sticks closer than a brother (Proverbs 18:24), that in all things God works for the good of those who love Him (Romans 8:28), and that we are secure in His hand (John 10:28). These are wonderful verses that provide us with hope and comfort. But we may have the tendency to interpret them as if we, as Christians, have immunity to life's trials. This is a distortion of the whole of Scripture as we are not promised "life on the easy track." In fact, it seems just the opposite. We are promised that we will "face trials of many kinds" (James 1:2). Yet we are disillusioned and surprised when they happen to us. Never in my wildest dreams did I imagine I would be in this situation, coping with the suicide of my eldest son. At times, I still cannot believe it has really happened. I subconsciously believed that God would immunize me as His child (and Shawn as His child) from such a terrible event, that He would never allow such a thing to happen. I was wrong. My perceptions of how God works were wrong and unscriptural. I guess I knew this all along in my head, but in my heart I expected to be protected from such a horrible tragedy.

God allows the natural course of events to unfold in this fallen and sinful world. Our spiritual standing may have nothing to do with what happens. The quality of our Christian walk may be unrelated to events in our lives. As I stated earlier, it may be eternity before "all things work together for good." As we examine the early church, many were martyred, not because they were unfaithful to their Lord, but just the opposite—because they were faithful. Virtually all the apostles were killed for their beliefs. Job, a righteous man, suffered terribly through no fault of his own. The quality of our Christian life may have no correlation to trials we suffer in this life. I struggle with this as it seems so unjust and unfair. It is only then I realize that I do not have all the knowledge and cannot see what God can see. Like Job, I cry for answers but must be content, at times, with God's silence, knowing He has the answers even if I do not. I would prefer God to cover Christians with a security blanket that would protect us from the terrible consequences of living in a sinful world. That is not the case. Perhaps James gives us a glimpse of why. He states that we will have trials (James 1:2) but also notes that those trials will strengthen our faith (v. 3), build our character (v. 3,4), allow for God's gift of wisdom as our faith matures (vv. 5,6) and finally we receive his crown of life which allows for blessedness in this life and also in the life to come (v. 12). Perhaps what God wishes us to know is that our hope, comfort, joy, peace and security are not rooted in present circumstances but in His constant presence and His grace, wisdom and strength. While not cloistering us from life's hardship, He equips us to endure them.

His Sustaining Presence

While God has not promised the Christian a life of ease and comfort, He has promised that He will never leave us or forsake us (Deuteronomy 31:6; Hebrews 13:5). The hope of the Christian is not found in answers to all life's problems or protection from the pain of living in this fallen world. It is in the constant presence of God, promised to us by the Father Himself. His care and love for us was supremely demonstrated in sending Christ, His Son, to be our Saviour. Any doubt about God's provision was answered once and for all at Calvary. Like the psalmist, we must all go through the valley of the shadow of death, but we need fear no evil, as His rod and staff will comfort us (Psalm 23). Note that we are not protected from going through the valley but are promised His presence as we go through it.

This flies in the face of much of the prosperity gospel we hear today which implies that, if we just trust God, He will supply all our desires and wants. The Bible never promises to meet all our wants, just our needs. I think many of us have drastically confused the two. When David the psalmist was granted the "desire of his heart" (Psalm 21:2), it was in the context of a heart rejoicing in the strength of his Lord (v. 1) and fully trusting in the unfailing love of God (v. 7). The very idea that God grants the carnal desires of the human heart is ludicrous. Indeed, those desires lead to destruction and "come to nothing" (Psalm 112:10). Our heavenly Father knows our needs even before we ask, but we are still to ask. However, the Father is the judge of what is best for us as He only gives good gifts to His children (Matthew 7:11; Luke 11:13; John 14:13,14). The receiving of God's "good" gifts is in the context of faith in Christ (John 14:12), asking in the name of Christ which also brings glory to God (John 14:13) and a love for Christ that results in obedience to His commands (John 14:15) with God still defining what is in our best interests. A smooth, bountiful, trouble-free life is never promised to the Christian, more the opposite (James 1:2).

I wish with all my heart that I would have been protected from the pain of Shawn's untimely death. God, in His wisdom, did not see fit to do that. He allowed the events to unfold with the painful consequences that followed. But His presence has been with us every step of the way, sustaining, encouraging, comforting and strengthening. As I shared previously, He has met our needs, primarily through His people. Although the burden has seemed too much to bear at times, through His grace we have survived. Like Job, we have not been given the answers or understand why such a terrible thing happened, but His presence has not been withdrawn and He asks for our trust and confidence, even in our darkest times. I believe He was with Shawn even at that terrible, confused time of his death, not approving of what he was doing but being true to His promise not to leave or forsake.

I have pondered this time and time again. How could God be with Shawn and not prevent his drastic action? In fact, was Shawn's faith a contributing factor to his death? Being with his Lord and Saviour was preferred to continuing to live in this world. I know that obedience is crucial to the life of the Christian, and Shawn was disobeying God's revealed will when he took his life, but in his mind, he saw his death as a release from the cares of this world. That is not hard to understand. Even the Apostle Paul wished for death to release him from this sinful world (Philippians 1:23). David wished for his death over his son, Absalom's untimely demise (2 Samuel 18:33). Life's events can certainly make any of us lose our perspective. That does not give us permission to take a life, but it does help us understand some of the context that results in such an act.

Why God did not empower Shawn to cope with the things in his life that led to his death, I do not know. Perhaps the responsibility rests on Shawn for not asking, or perhaps some physical or mental impairment prevented him for reaching out at that moment. We will never know in this life. What we can know is that God's presence was not withdrawn as God cannot break His promise. I need to remind myself of this constantly and call on my heavenly Father to sustain me each moment of the day. His faithfulness is a given on which we can rely. This confidence in His constant presence allows us to live each new day, no matter how difficult, with purpose and hope.

Chapter 8

Continuing to Cope in Today's World

THE WORLD in which we live is alien to a Christian perspective. It is, in many ways, hostile to the notion that we have a creator to whom we are responsible. I have pondered how different the world of my children and students is from the world in which I was a youth. And, while the postmodern world may have increased technological advantages, it is a world, I believe, much more impersonal and less caring than that of a generation ago. A personal God to whom we give an account is disappearing. As Colson points out (Colson, 1999), we don't just live together in a world, having differing opinions that don't really make much of a difference. Instead, we see the emergence of clashing worldviews where a materialistic, naturalistic view, opposed to biblical Christianity, now dominates the scene. The moral boundaries that were accepted by most in the community in which I grew up are no longer seen as relevant. No longer does a postmodern world accept a universal, absolute truth as a reality. It is now all relative. I fear for a generation that no longer believes in limits originating from the Creator of the world in which we all exist.

We are caught between these two clashing worldviews. On the one hand, for example, my students are taught at ABU that all truth is God's truth and true learning is discovering God's truth in His Word and His world. Conversely, the world tells them such a notion is a myth and that we are all part of a chance existence with no real meaning apart from that. It is not surprising there is so much confusion and insecurity among our population today. Material well-being is the overriding goal of society rather than loving service to the God of creation and those created in His image. The mixed messages received, especially by our youth, are very perplexing for them. They are told that wealth, prosperity and power are the worthwhile goals to strive for, even at the expense of others, while also hearing we are to "love our neighbour as ourselves." It is not hard to see which goal is winning.

Christians are not immunized from such clashes. Indeed, as Colson notes, we have bought into the materialistic view with a vengeance. As I look back, I am so much more aware now of the pressures and conflicts Shawn must have been enduring as he attempted to cope with a world that measured him by materialistic standards while he struggled with his commitment to the Lord and all that involved in terms of who he was and what was really important. I believe it is a common dilemma experienced by many Christian young people. They must cope with clashing standards of what is worthwhile in this life. The "good life" rather than the "committed, sacrificial life" beckons with much more vigor and attraction. It puts tremendous pressure on young people today to achieve success as defined by the materialistic world. However, a world run by greed and power-broking is not concerned with the welfare of the individual caught in its web. Consequently, the materialistic goal set forth by society as worthy is unattainable for many as the few in power consolidate their position at the expense of the many.

As Colson states:

> The real war is a cosmic struggle between worldviews—between the Christian worldview and the various secular and spiritual worldviews arrayed against it (Colson, 1999:17).

While noting the influence of many of the naturalistic worldviews including Darwinism, modernism, postmodernism, New Age and Marxism, I feel he neglects to give adequate treatment to perhaps the most insidious of them all—modern capitalism. Much of the world is now controlled by a system based upon greed, maximum profits for the stockholders and the consolidation of power in the hands of a few. Increased economic globalization is a fact of life, and materialistic factors override all others in much of today's world.

Researching and writing a paper on "Power, Wealth & Greed—Disturbing Trends and a Christian Response" has been a troubling experience for me. As I examined the growing concentration of wealth and power in our society, the growing gap between the wealthy and the poor, the decline in the real standard of living of the working people during the eighties and nineties and the slashing of jobs by major corporations in order to increase short-term profits for the wealthy stockholders, I became increasingly distressed. This is the world our young people are moving into, and it is demoralizing and discouraging for many of them. They witness greed, selfishness, lack of integrity, dishonesty and corruption at the highest levels of our society. I realized that this is the world that impacted Shawn in very negative ways. He wanted very much to be a success in his business, to achieve in the business-world milieu. Yet he knew the priorities of the Christian faith. I'm sure I underestimated the conflict he was going through. I also don't believe we can conveniently separate the macro (societal) and micro (personal) variables that influence our lives. We are products of both, and they interact with each other in very complex ways. The clash between the naturalistic and Christian worldviews is very real in our world.

Important Learning from this Experience

I have been taught much by what has happened to our family. Although I would gladly trade it all if I could reverse what has happened, nevertheless, important teachings have resulted which have had a profound impact on me. In conclusion, I would like to review some of them.

The Comfort and Sustaining Power of Faith

As I look back on what has happened and the horror of what we have been through, I shudder to think what it would have been like without my faith in the Lord. Although some may consider faith a crutch on which we prop ourselves up in times of adversity, I really don't see the problem with that. We absolutely need a crutch at times, and I was so grateful to have one as I would have been lost without it. Whether we admit it or not, we all live by faith. The only difference is the object in which we place that faith. Some place their faith in science, some in physical ability, some in a particular philosophy and others in material possessions. In the end, we all live by faith. What we need to examine is the validity of the object in which we have placed our faith. Although I initially wrestled spiritually with how a Christian could come to the place of suicide and God allow it, I'm thankful His grace was sufficient and sustained me even in my doubts and confusion.

The Christian faith is placed in the reality of a sovereign God, creator of the universe, who has proved Himself throughout history, supremely in the gift of His son, Jesus, who provided the means for a fallen world to be reconciled to God. The comfort and strength God has provided for us through this terrible ordeal has been marvelous. It has been the source of much security and hope, without which my distress would have been so much worse. Knowing the presence of a loving God was with us throughout this time of so much anguish was a great comfort. His everlasting arms have not let us down. I wonder how people cope with such tragedy without the hope and solace that come from a vital faith in the Comforter. It is this faith that allows us to live in hope even when the circumstances seem so hopeless.

God's Provision—Family and Friends

My appreciation for how family and friends are instrumental in providing support in such a horrible time has been greatly expanded. I read this quote recently on some stationary: "God meets us in the heart of a friend." How true we have found this to be. I cannot find words to express how grateful I have been to family and friends for their wonderful care of us over the last three-and-a-half years. I thank God every day for His marvelous provision for us in such a loving group of people who have put hands and feet to their love in so many ways.

Changing Priorities

Shawn's death has made me rethink my priorities like nothing else has. Facing the death of one so close and so young hammers home the message of just how tenuous and uncertain life really is. We have no guarantees of tomorrow. The reality of my own mortality has been pressed upon me like a thunderbolt. We really are, as Scripture declares, like grass that is here today and tomorrow is withered away. As we get older, we look back over our lives and are amazed at how fast the years have gone. Looking back over the few short years we had Shawn with us, it seems like the blink of an eye. As my mind has been bombarded with the shortness of life, much of what I used to think was important and worth getting upset over now no longer affects me much. Material things, career accomplishments, personal agendas, although not unimportant, have diminished in my perception, and other things like strengthening my walk with the Lord, reinforcing relationships and deepening my commitment to a service mentality rather than an "acquiring" mentality, have gained a new importance.

When you lose a child, those things with eternal significance really take on a whole new dimension.

> Finally, brothers, whatever is true, whatever is noble, whatever is right, whatever is pure, whatever is lovely, whatever is admirable—if anything is excellent or praiseworthy— think about such things (Philippians 4:8).

This verse has taken on a whole new meaning for me. I hope Neil's statement that this experience must make us more loving people will prove prophetic in the lives of each of us as a family, both to each other within our family circle and also to others outside in the larger community.

Increased Ministry Opportunities—the Role of Service in Healing

We have slowly discovered that even such a terrible tragedy can have positive aspects. Because of the deep pain we have gone through, it has taken some time before we have had the strength to reach out to others uniquely because of our experience. But it has and is happening. We are not the only people to have suffered such anguish and loss, and we can now, as it were, emotionally wrap our arms of comfort and support around other grieving family members as ones who have "been there." I am discovering that unique experiences allow unique ministry opportunities. There is relevance to the concept of the "wounded healer." I can relate on a level never before open to me as the result of Shawn's death and walk through doors of opportunity with a credibility not previously possessed. It does not compensate for what has happened but does allow some good to emerge from the horrible bad.

It has also been part of my healing to be able to reach out to others from my own brokenness. One of the most therapeutic things you can do to facilitate your own healing is to reach out to someone else. I have had opportunities to counsel, speak, write, share, both with individuals and groups, my grief journey, and use my own healing experiences to assist others. If God's faithfulness in my life during such a painful time can encourage someone else, who may be suffering similarly, in their faith walk, I will be grateful for that outcome.

The Greatest is Love

We have all heard that "love makes the world go round." The importance of love in human relations cannot be overstated. The loss of Shawn has impressed on me the significance of love in ways I previously had not considered. I have realized in a new way how deep love can go. Our love for Shawn was so strong that his loss penetrated the very depths of our beings with anguish like we had never felt before. It also made me realize just how much I love Neil and Jaclyn as even the thought of losing them created in me such extreme fear and apprehension. Experiencing the love of close friends and family has also influenced me in life-changing ways. Because of their loving care for us, my appreciation has increased beyond measure of how priceless and incredible is this thing called love. I have been deeply challenged to put this loving service into practice in my own life.

I gained a whole new appreciation of how much God must love us to sacrifice His own Son for us. It is so much more than an emotion as it encompasses our whole reality as humans. As Scripture states, "And now these three remain: faith, hope and love. But the greatest of these is love" (1 Corinthians 13:13).

Conclusion

I HAVE FOUND the writing of this account both debilitating and therapeutic. As I have recounted the circumstances of Shawn's death, it has reopened deep wounds of anguish and grief. Time after time, I have relived those dreadful moments and felt over again the stabbing knives of pain, despair, horror and shock. There were times I regretted even starting such an under-taking. My heart longed for the temporary relief that comes from avoidance. My head, however, knew that, in the end, this exercise would strengthen and increase my coping ability. Thank goodness my head won out in this instance. I am stronger now for having gone through this process. I have emerged from the darkness of despair much better equipped to live in the light of hope, which earlier did not even seem a possibility.

I also pray this account will prove helpful to others who have suffered great loss. I have no magic solutions, no profound saying which will eliminate the pain. I can just share our anguish and how we have survived, allowing us to now face life with more confidence and assurance. Although we will never completely fill the hole in our lives resulting from the loss of Shawn, we now know that life for us can go on, that we can recapture some of the joy of living, that all is not lost and that purpose and living a worthwhile existence are possible. If it is possible for us, it is possible for others. I want to encourage each person who has faced such a terrible loss to seek out help, both from people and God, to believe in your own inner strength, to look beyond the past and face the future as a new person for that you will surely be. Such events change us forever. While we may curse the situation that precipitated the change, we can still embrace those new characteristics in our lives that now provide strength, resilience, determination, courage and hope. We have emerged scarred but not destroyed from life's worst pit. That is surely worth something, for which I thank my Lord.

Appendix

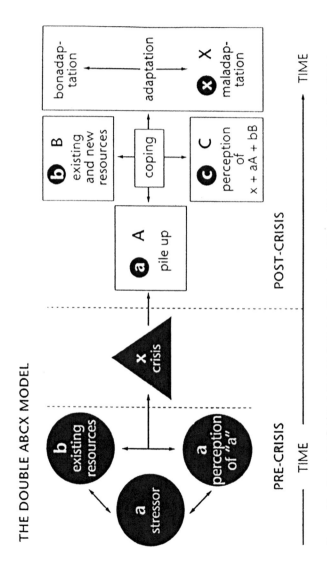

THE DOUBLE ABCX MODEL

Source: Hamilton I. McCubbin & Joan M. Patterson, "Family Transitions: Adaptation to Stress" In Hamilton I. McCubbin & Charles R. Figley (1983). *Stress and the Family. Volume 1: Coping with Normative Transitions*. New York: Brunner/Mazel, p. 12.

Bibliography

Barnes, M. Craig. *When God Interrupts.* Downers Grove, Illinois: Inter-Varsity Press, 1996.

Blackburn, Bill and Deana Mattingly. *Caring in Times of Family Crisis.* Nashville: Convention Press, 1987.

Bolton, Iris. "Death of a Child by Suicide." In T.A. Rando (Ed.), *Parental Loss of a Child.* Champaign, Illinois: Research Press, 1986: pp. 5-43.

Byers, Dale A. *Suicide: How God Sustained a Family.* Schaumburg, Illinois: Regular Baptist Press, 1991.

Colson, Charles and Nancy Pearcey. *How Now Shall We Live?* Wheaton, Illinois: Tyndale House, 1999.

Evenson, Brad. *Suicide Linked to Defective Gene.* National Post, Vol. 2, No. 81, January 28, 2000.

Gorman, Christine. "Suicide Check." *TIME* Domestic, Vol. 144, No. 22, November 28, 1994.

Health and Welfare Canada. *Suicide in Canada.* Report of the National Task Force on Suicide in Canada, Ottawa: Dept. of National Health and Welfare, 1987.

James, John W. and Russell Friedman. *The Grief Recovery Handbook*. New York: HarperCollins, 1998.

Lenzkes, Susan. *When Life Takes What Matters*. Grand Rapids, Michigan: Discovery House, 1993 (www.time.com/time/magazine/archive/1994).

Leutwyler, Kristin. "Suicide Prevention." *Scientific American*, March, 1997 (www.sciam.com/0397issue/0397scicit1.html).

Lewis, C.S. *A Grief Observed*. New York: Seabury Press, 1961.

Packer, J.I. *Knowing God*. Toronto: Hodder and Stoughton, 1973.

Pangrazzi, Arnaldo. *Bearing the Special Grief of Suicide*. St. Meinrad, Indiana: Abby Press, 1988.

Rando, Therese A. "The Unique Issues and Impact of a Death of a Child." In T.A. Rando (Ed.), *Parental Loss of a Child*. Champaign, Illinois: Research Press, 1986, pp. 5-43.

Rando, Therese A. "Parental Bereavement: An Exception to the General Conceptualizations of Mourning." In T.A. Rando (Ed.), *Parental Loss of a Child*. Champaign, Illinois: Research Press, 1986, pp. 45-58.

Rando, Therese A. (Ed.) *Parental Loss of a Child*. Champaign, Illinois: Research Press, 1986.

Rando, Therese A. *Grief, Dying, and Death: Clinical Interventions for Caregivers*. Champaign, Illinois: Research Press, 1984.

Samuel, Dorothy T. *Grieving: An Inward Journey*. St. Cloud, Minnesota: North Star Press, 1987.

Schatz, Barbara D. "Grief of Mothers." In T.A. Rando (Ed.). *Parental Loss of a Child*. Champaign, Illinois: Research Press, 1986, pp. 303-314.

Schatz, William H. "Grief of Fathers." In T.A. Rando (Ed.), *Parental Loss of a Child*. Champaign, Illinois: Research Press, 1986, pp.293-302.

Sproul, R.C. *Reason to Believe*. Grand Rapids, Michigan: Lamplighter Books, 1982.

Strommen, Merton P. and Irene A. Strommen. *Five Cries of Grief*. San Francisco: Harper, 1993.

Swanson, Steve. *Bible Readings for Men*. Minneapolis, Minnesota: Augsburg, 1984.

Swindoll, Charles R. *The Quest for Character.* Portland, Oregon: Multnomah Press, 1987.

Swindoll, Charles R. *Growing Deep in the Christian Life.* Portland, Oregon: Multnomah Press, 1986.

Swindoll, Charles R. *Growing Strong in the Seasons of Life.* Portland, Oregon: Multnomah Press, 1983.

Tagliaferre, Lewis and Gary L. Harbaugh. *Recovery from Loss.* Deerfield Beach, Florida: Health Communications, 1990.

Tengbom, Mildred. *Grief for a Season.* Minneapolis, Minnesota: Bethany House, 1989.

Yancey, Philip. *The Jesus I Never Knew.* Grand Rapids, Michigan: Zondervan, 1995.

Yancey, Philip. *Disappointment with God.* Grand Rapids, Michigan: Zondervan, 1988.

Wolterstorff, Nicholas. *Lament for a Son.* Grand Rapids, Michigan: William B. Eerdmans, 1987.

Web Sites

Lamenting Sons: Fathers and Grief. Available from http://www.members.tripod.com/LifeGard/index–4.html; accessed 1/16/2001.

SA\ VE CDC Statistics Page. CDC–National Center for Injury Prevention and Control. Available from http://www.save.org/cdcstat1.html; accessed 1/17/2001.

Suicide in the United States. National Center for Injury Prevention and Control, Home Page. Available from http://www.cdc.gov/ncipc/factsheets/suifacts.htm; accessed 1/16/2001.

Suicide, The Death No One Talks About. *Pine Rest Today.* Ed.V.N. Engeltjes, 2001. Available from http://www.pinerest.org/library/todays/prtsuic.htm; accessed 1/17/2001.

The Suicide Paradigm. Available from http://www.members.tripod.com/LifeGard/index..html; accessed 1/16/2001.

The Surgeon General's Call to Action to Prevent Suicide, 1999. Available from http://www.surgeongeneral.gov/library/calltoaction/fact3.htm; accessed 1/16/2001.

When the Worst Has Happened. Available from http://www.save.org/worst.html; accessed 1/17/2001.

Printed in the United States
78511LV00002B/16

9 781553 064909